NUTSHELLS

LAND LAW
IN A NUTSHELL

FOURTH EDITION

by

William Howarth,
former Deputy Director
School of Professional and Continuing Education
University of Hong Kong

London • Sweet & Maxwell • 1997

First edition 1987
Second edition 1991
Third edition 1994
Reprinted 1997
Fourth edition 1997

Published in 1997 by
Sweet & Maxwell Limited of
100 Avenue Road, London NW3 3PF
Phototypeset by
Wyvern 21 Limited, Bristol
Printed in England by Clays Ltd., St Ives plc

A CIP Catalogue record
for this book is available
from the British Library

ISBN 0–421–595906

©
Sweet & Maxwell
1997

NUTSHELLS

LAND LAW

IN A NUTSHELL

FARNHAM college

AUSTRALIA
LBC Information Services
Sydney

CANADA and USA
Carswell
Toronto

NEW ZEALAND
Brooker's
Auckland

SINGAPORE and MALAYSIA
Thomson Information (S.E. Asia)
Singapore

CONTENTS

1. INTRODUCTORY TOPICS

CLASSIFICATION OF PROPERTY

English law

English law makes a primary distinction between real and personal property (realty and personalty). This distinction corresponds in the main to the distinction drawn in civil law systems between immovable and movable property, though the peculiar English history of leases provides an exception.

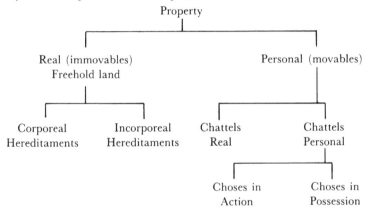

1. Real property. Originally, real property was the term applied to any property that was the subject-matter of a real action in the common law courts. This applied only to freehold interests in land and was not available to actions relating to leaseholds. In terms of land a distinction should be drawn between corporeal hereditaments, which are inheritable rights capable of being physically possessed, *i.e.* the land and buildings themselves as compared with incorporeal hereditaments, which are inheritable rights in land which cannot be possessed, *e.g.* easements.

2. Personal property. This relates to any property which could be made the subject of a personal action, the action being against the individual rather than the property. The consequence of a personal action, *e.g.* for dispossession, was that the wrongful dispossessor could either hand back the personal property or pay compensation, whereas with a real action, if a freeholder had been dispossessed wrongly, then possession of the property had to be handed back.

3. Chattels Real (leases). Historically, leases were treated as personal property because only a personal action could be taken for dispossession in the courts. Today a lease is capable of being a legal estate in land (term of years absolute), hence the term "chattels real," such property having a "mongrel amphibious nature"— Blackstone.

4. Chattels personal. Covers all other personal property and can be subdivided into choses in action and choses in possession. A chose in action is an intangible right which can only be claimed or enforced by action and not be taking physical possession, *e.g.* the right to collect a debt; or the proceeds of a cheque; patents; copyright; company stocks and shares. Such assets are capable of being sold, pledged and transferred. A chose in possession is a tangible right that can be enjoyed by taking possession of the thing, *e.g.* car; book; furniture. Whether property is classified as real or personal although mainly of historical interest, it is still significant in matters of probate, *e.g.* if in a will a person leaves all his realty to X and all his personalty to Y. In relation to the doctrine of conversion, see *Williams & Glyn's v. Boland* (1981) and in the context of leases, section 2 of the Law of Property (Miscellaneous Provisions) Act 1989.

Land as a legal concept

1. In the physical sense land includes not only the ground, soil or earth, but also all buildings on the land, any fixtures attached thereto, mines and minerals and any incorporeal rights such as easements. Subject to certain exceptions (see post) land includes the sub-soil down to the depths of the earth and the airspace above the land up to a reasonable height: Law of Property Act 1925, s.205(1)(ix).

2. All land in England is technically owned by the Crown, dating back to the time of the conquest in 1066, when William the Conqueror claimed ownership of all land in England by right of conquest. From that time the doctrine that all land is held directly or indirectly of the Crown was established. For this reason it is inappropriate to describe the individual occupier of land as the owner. Ownership is commonly thought of as indicating certain rights over a piece of property such as a chattel. These rights

include the right to possession, the right to enjoy and the right of disposition. A further feature of land occupation is that it has always been recognised that these ownership rights need not be vested in the same person, *e.g.* where a trust exists, or where there are a number of different estates in the same piece of land. It is consequently more appropriate to deal with a person's right to possession (seisin), rather than ownership, in determining title to land.

Fixtures and fittings

1. "Land" includes any object which is attached to the land so as to form part of it. Consequently when a chattel is affixed to land or to a building, it may become a fixture and form part of the land itself. This is of importance in deciding whether a land-owner, on selling or leasing property, can remove the object. The problem may further arise in connection with mortgages, devises and settlements. If a chattel has not become a fixture, it is known as a fitting.

2. In determining whether a chattel has become a fixture, a combination of two tests are applied:
   (a) the degree of annexation;
   (b) the purpose of annexation.

3. The degree of annexation. Unless actually fastened or con-nected with the land or building in a substantial way a chattel cannot normally become a fixture. A test often applied is whether the item can be removed without causing damage. In *Elwes v. Maw* (1802), a dutch barn resting on sockets let into the ground was held not to be a fixture. Where an article merely rests of its own weight on the land, it is not, prima facie, a fixture: *Hulme v. Bright-man* (1943), however this may be rebutted when it is clear that the object was intended as a permanent improvement of the land: *Berkeley v. Poulet* (1976)—marble plinth resting of its own weight was a fixture, though the marble statue on the top was not: *cf. Dean v. Andrews* (1985), a prefabricated greenhouse bolted to a concrete plinth which rested of its own weight on the ground was not held to be a fixture.

4. The purpose of annexation. Where the purpose of attaching a chattel is to permanently improve the land, rather than merely to display the chattel, then a fixture is presumed. Even if the degree of attachment is substantial the chattel may not become a fixture if the method of fixing was necessary for its proper enjoyment: *Leigh v. Taylor* (1902)—tapestries affixed by nails and tacks were not fixtures: *cf. Vaudeville Electric Co. v. Muriset* (1923)—cinema seats secured to the ground were held to be fixtures. Objects such as statues, seats and ornamental vases have been held to be fixtures even though they are only held in position by their own weight, the reason being that they formed part of the architectural design of a house of grounds: *Re Whaley* (1968). A recent review of the principles applicable to fixtures and fittings occurred in *Botham v. T.S.B.* (1996), where the court held that fitted kitchen units were fixtures, but that a freezer fitted under a worktop, an oven fitted into the kitchen units, an integrated dishwasher, an integrated washing machine and dryer and a refrigerator fitted under the worktop were not fixtures.

5. Exceptions. As a general rule if an item constitutes a fixture it cannot be removed from the land. There are however certain limited exceptions to this rule:

(a) Landlord and Tenant: a tenant for years may remove certain "tenants fixtures" during the lease, or within a reasonable time thereafter.

These include:

   (i) trade fixtures;
   (ii) ornamental and domestic fixtures;
   (iii) agricultural fixtures.

(b) Mortgagor and mortgagee: the mortgagor cannot remove fixtures during the course of the mortgage.

(c) Tenant for life and remaindermen: approximately the same as with landlord and tenant.

(d) Personal representatives and devisee: the recipient of a gift of land by will is entitled to fixtures. Personal representatives may not remove fixtures.

2. THE DOCTRINE OF TENURES AND ESTATES

THE DOCTRINE OF TENURES

Introduction

From the time of the Norman conquest (and even for several centuries before, on a limited scale) English land law adopted the continental system of feudalism (hierarchy dominated by a sovereign or chief and based on mutual promises of protection and military service). William the Conqueror 1066–87 regarded the whole of England as his by conquest and granted land, not by out and out transfer, but to be held of him as overlord. Persons holding land of the Crown might then grant land to another (subinfeudate) to hold of him in return for services. The feudal pyramid that was constructed was based upon the land tenure system. The tenure of the land identifying the conditions on which land was held. Tenure was the main bond holding society together, the lord protecting those who held land of him.

Forms of tenure

1. Free tenures. Where the nature of the duties were fixed, and the services were rendered freely. The most common types of free tenure were:

(a) lay tenures of a chivalrous nature such as knight's service (military service in return for land) or grand sergeantry (personal services for the king);

(b) common socage: agricultural tenure of a fixed nature;

(c) spiritual tenure such as frankalmoign and divine service, which involved grants to ecclesiastical bodies in return for the saying of prayers or masses for the repose of the soul of the lord and for his spiritual wellbeing.

2. Unfree tenures. Villeinage or copyhold: these were services of a servile nature, often agricultural, but not fixed in nature and amount. By the fourteenth century these were commuted to payment of rent, enabling the lord to hire labour independently.

Incidents of tenure

As part of the tenure system the lord was entitled to certain incidents which were often of real value to him. These varied with the different types of tenure held. The most common incidents were:

(a) Homage, fealty and suit of court; this was the spiritual and temporal bond between the lord and his tenant, the tenant swearing to be the lord's man and to perform the feudal obligations as well as agreeing to attend the lord's court;

(b) Relief: money payments due when the tenant died;

(c) Aids: payments required when the lord needed ransom or the eldest son was knighted or his daughter needed dowry;

(d) Escheat and forfeiture: where the land passed to the lord because of failure of heirs or where the tenant committed a serious crime;

(e) Wardship: the right to retain profits from the land where the tenant was an infant;

(f) Marriage: the right to select the spouse of a tenant.

Effects of the tenure system today

In general the doctrine of tenures has no practical effect today. The Abolition of Tenures Act 1660 and Law of Property Act 1925 (L.P.A. 1925) abolished almost all incidents and forms of tenure. Consequently, there is now only one form of tenure, *i.e.* socage or freehold tenure as it is sometimes termed.

THE DOCTRINE OF ESTATES

The doctrine of tenures dealt with the conditions on which land was held. The doctrine of estates is concerned with the length of time for which land is held. Because all land in England is held of the Crown, English law has developed the concept of the estate which has its emphasis on the right to possession. An estate is an interest in land of defined duration, it is an abstract entity which represents the extent of a person's rights to possession (seisin).

Classification of estates

Estates vary in size according to their duration, the major distinction being between freehold and leasehold estates.

1. The general nature of these estates is considered below, though they are considered in further detail at appropriate places in the text.

2. There are two principal categories of estate, freehold and less than freehold. A freehold estate (originally deriving its origin from the law of tenures) is one whose duration is uncertain, whereas an

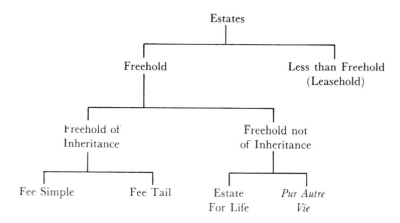

estate less than freehold is one for a period whose duration is fixed or capable of being fixed, *e.g.* a lease for 10 years.

Freehold estates

1. Fee simple. This is the largest estate in terms of duration and is as near to "absolute ownership" as it is possible to achieve. The word "fee" denotes inheritability, "simple" indicates that the estate is inheritable by general heirs, *i.e.* ascendants, descendants or collateral. The fee simple is virtually everlasting in that it continues as long as the person entitled for the time being has "heirs" at his death. The classic words of limitation used to create such an estate are "to X and his heirs".

2. Fee tail. An inheritable estate which lasts as long as the original grantee or any of his descendants live. The term "fee tail," "estate tail," "entail" or "entailed interest" are often used to describe the same estate. A classic method of creation was to use the words "to X and the heirs of his body." A restriction of the line of descendants to the male or female species only could be created by a "fee tail male" or a "fee tail female." Fee tails are rarely created and under the Trusts of Land and Appointment of Trustees Act 1996 (operative from January 1, 1997) it is no longer possible to create an entailed interest.

3. Life estate. A grant of an estate to the grantee for his life. The estate is not inheritable and can only exist as an equitable interest after 1925.

4. Estate pur autre vie. This is a species of life estate where the right to the estate exists for the duration of someone else's life. A grant of Blackacre "to X for the duration of Y's life" would create such an estate which terminates on Y's death.

Estates less than freehold

1. These were brought into the estate system in the 16th century and now comprise various forms of leasehold including:
   (a) fixed terms of certain duration, *e.g.* "to X for 99 years";
   (b) a term the duration of which is capable of being rendered certain, *e.g.* "to Y from year to year";
   (c) a tenancy at will; though the exact status of such a right is uncertain.

Estates in possession, remainder and reversion

1. A further consequence of the concept of the "estate" is that the law allows various smaller and simultaneous estates to be carved out of the fee simple estate: *e.g.* To A for life: B for life; C in fee simple.

2. An estate *in possession* is one where a present right to immediate enjoyment is given, *e.g.* there is no preceding estate to postpone enjoyment. In the above example the estate of A is in possession. Where land will revert back to the original grantor, then the grantor has an estate *in reversion* so that if Blackacre is conveyed by X "to A for life," then the estate of X is a reversion. In the grant to A for life; B for life; C in fee simple, the estate of B and C are estates *in remainder*, *i.e.* they do not have a present right to actual enjoyment, their right to possession being postponed to the future. The estate of A being in possession is known as a "particular estate."

The rights of a fee simple owner

The fee simple being the largest estate that can exist in land carries with it many of the rights associated with absolute ownership of property.

1. Natural rights. There is a natural right of support for land (though not buildings, which must be acquired by easement or covenant) and a natural right to an unpolluted free flow of air across property. These rights exist automatically and do not require any form of grant.

2. The right of alienation. A fee simple owner may dispose of his land in any way he chooses, either by deed or by will.

3. The right of enjoyment. The rights of enjoyment possessed by a fee simple owner are extensive. In physical terms he may enjoy everything on, beneath and above the land (*cujus est solum, ejus est usque ad coelum et ad inferos*), though there are practical restrictions to this rule.

Limitations on the rights of the fee simple owner

1. Limits of the land.
(a) sudden accretions from the sea of substantial size belong to the Crown, though gradual accretions belong to the owner;
(b) the foreshore (land between high and low water mark) belongs to the Crown unless otherwise specially granted;
(c) the airspace up to a reasonable height belongs to the owner; *Lord Bernstein of Leigh v. Skyways & Geneva Ltd* (1977) and if interfered with may give rise to an action in trespass or nuisance: *Kelsen v. Imperial Tobacco Co.* (1957). Under the Civil Aviation Act 1949 no action can be taken in respect of aircraft that pass over property at a reasonable height. In *Anchor Brewhouse Developments Ltd v. Berkley House (Docklands Developments) Ltd* (1987) an injunction was granted to prevent the jib of a crane swinging over adjoining property as this amounted to a trespass.

2. Rights of others over land. Examples include easements, mortgages and leases.

3. Statutory restrictions. Various statutes particularly over the last 60 or 70 years have eroded away certain rights of an owner. Many of these statutes are based on public interest and illustrate public authority interference. Examples include Town and Country Planning Acts; Rent Acts; and Housing and Public Health Acts.

4. Treasure. The well known principle of treasure trove has been replaced with a new set of principles under the Treasure Act 1996. The definition of treasure is much wider than the common law definition of treasure trove and includes all finds of major historical significance. When treasure is found it will vest in the franchisee, if there is one, otherwise in the Crown. Coroners will still hold inquests to determine whether items found constitute treasure, but in most cases without a jury. The Department of National Heritage will produce a new code of practice for dealing with rewards to finders of treasure.

5. Minerals. These belong to the tenant at common law but statute has considerably reduced these rights so that gold and silver in mines belongs to the Crown and most valuable minerals such as coal or petroleum are similarly vested therein.

6. Wild animals. These cannot form the subject-matter of ownership, but a fee simple owner has a qualified right to catch, kill and appropriate. Certain species of animals and birds are however protected by statute, *e.g.* Wildlife and Countryside Act 1981.

7. Liability in tort. In exercising rights over land the fee simple owner must not interfere with the legal rights of others. Consequently liability in tort may arise:
   (a) where a nuisance is caused, *e.g.* smells or noise;
   (b) under the rule in *Rylands v. Fletcher* (1868), *e.g.* where water escapes.

8. Fishing rights. In non-tidal waters the owner has the exclusive right to fish though this right may be granted to others, *e.g.* fishing clubs. In tidal water, the public has a right to fish up to the point of ebb and flow of the tide.

9. Water rights. The right to extract water which flows or percolates through land is governed by the Water Resources act 1991. The basic rule is that a licence from the National Rivers Authority must be obtained for any extraction of water from any source, *i.e.* percolating or from a defined channel. No licence is required in the case of abstractions of small quantities of water for certain limited authorised purposes, *e.g.* domestic purposes of the occupiers household or agricultural purposes other than spray irrigation.

10. River beds. The owner of land through which a non tidal river flows owns the river bed. Where a river separates two plots of land, each plot owner owns the bed up to the middle. Tidal rivers belong to the Crown.

11. Chattels found on the land. In general the owner of land of which he is in control has the best claim to valuable items found under or attached to the land where the true owner cannot be found; *Parker v. British Airways Board* (1982). Where an item is found on the surface of the land, the finder may have a better claim. The position becomes more complicated when the finder is a trespasser. In *Waverley B.C. v. Fletcher* (1995) a person used a metal detector to unearth a valuable brooch in a public park owned by the local authority and it was held that the landowner had a better claim than the finder. Metal detection involving digging up and removing property was not a permitted public recreational use and constituted trespass.

---

3. LAW AND EQUITY

Introduction

Because of the deficiencies of the common law as administered in early common law courts, *i.e.* delay, complicated procedures of the writ system and inadequate remedies, a body of law known as equity was developed by the Court of Chancery giving a new range of rights and remedies to assist a potential litigant. It was in the realms of property law that equity made its greatest contribution.

Rights created by equity

1. The Trust (use): at common law if property was transferred by a grantor to persons to hold (trustees) for the benefit of others (beneficiaries), the trustees were not bound to administer the trust property for the beneficiary's benefit. Equity, however, compelled the trustees to administer the trust in accordance with their conscience and if they defaulted they were liable for penalties.

2. The Equity of Redemption: the right of a mortgagor to redeem his property even after the legal redemption date (see below, Chap. 9).

3. Restrictive Covenants: the shortcomings in the law of covenants was mitigated by equity in the creation of the restrictive covenant, a development which can usually be traced to the decision in *Tulk v. Moxhay* (1848) (see below, Chap. 11).

Special remedies granted in equity

1. Injunction: an order compelling or restraining a person's actions.

2. Specific Performance: an order of the court compelling performance of an obligation, usually where damages are inappropriate.

3. Rescission: an order cancelling an obligation and restoring the parties to their original position.

4. Rectification: the court may order a contract to be altered where such contract is drawn up by common mistake and does not represent the true intention of the parties.

5. Certain new procedures were also introduced by equity, the most significant being *subpoena*, discovery of documents and interrogatories.

Legal and equitable rights

1. A legal right is a right *in rem* (in the thing itself) which is enforceable against the whole world. An equitable right is a right *in personam*, enforceable against certain persons only, *e.g.* it may not bind a bona fide purchaser for value of a legal estate who has no notice of the equitable interest.

2. The extent to which a purchaser is bound by third party rights when acquiring property is often determined by the nature of those rights, *i.e.* whether they are equitable or legal.

Example. If A and B are adjoining landowners and B grants to A by deed the perpetual right to cross his land to reach a main road then the nature of the right which A possessed is a legal easement: (see L.P.A. 1925, s.1(2)(*a*)). If B sells his land to a purchaser, C, then C will automatically be bound by the easement because it is a legal right enforcement against all persons. Had A granted the easement to B in writing, or merely to be exercised for B's lifetime, the nature of the right becomes equitable, and whether such right would bind C depends upon the doctrine of notice, (as amended by the principles of registration after 1925, see below, Chap. 4), the equitable right being a right *in personam*. The creation of legal rights depends upon the terms of L.P.A. 1925, s.1 (see below, Chap. 4).

The doctrine of notice

The basic doctrine of notice provides that an equitable interest will bind all persons other than "equity's darling," *i.e.* the bona fide purchaser for value of the legal estate with no notice of the equitable interest, or anyone who claims through him: *Pilcher v. Rawlins* (1872). The essential features of the doctrine are:

1. Bona fide. The purchase must act in good faith, *i.e.* there must be no fraud or sharp practices: *Midland Bank v. Green* (1980), though usually it merely serves to emphasise that the purchaser must be innocent as to notice.

2. Purchaser. Includes any person who takes the property by sale, mortgage, lease or otherwise, but excludes any acquisition by operation of law.

3. Value. Includes any consideration for money or money's worth or marriage (future), but not "good consideration": natural love and affection is not sufficient.

4. Of a legal estate. The estate purchased must be a legal estate, so that if the purchaser only has an equitable interest, then even if he has no notice he is bound by any prior equitable interests, because equity operates on the principle that where the equities are equal the first in time prevails: *McCarthy and Stone v. Julian S. Hodge Ltd* (1971). A purchaser without notice does not have to take a legal estate in order to take free from a "mere equity": *Westminster Bank v. Lee* (1956).

5. Without notice. Notice may be either actual, constructive or imputed:
   (a) *actual notice*: a purchaser has actual notice of all matters that have been brought to his attention, but not of facts that have come to his attention by way of vague rumours. Rights that are registrable in the Land Charges Register and are registered constitute actual notice: section 198 of L.P.A. 1925 (see below, Chap. 4).
   (b) *constructive notice*: a purchaser is under an obligation to undertake a full investigation of title before completing his purchase. He can only plead absence of notice if he made all usual and proper inquiries and has still found nothing to indicate the equitable interest. If he does not do so, or is careless or negligent, he is deemed to have "constructive notice" of all the matters he would have discovered: section 199 of L.P.A. 1925. The purchaser should:
      (i) inspect land and make inquiries as to anything which appears inconsistent with the title offered by the vendor: *Hunt v. Luck* (1902). Occupation of the property by some other person may amount to notice: *Hodgson v. Marks* (1971). As to the nature of inquiries to be made see: *Williams & Glyns Bank Ltd v. Boland* (1980); *Midland Bank Ltd v. Farm Pride Hatcheries Ltd* (1981); *Kingsnorth v. Tizard* (1986).
      (ii) investigate title for at least the last 15 years by way of the title deeds. The purchaser is deemed to have notice

of any equitable rights recorded on the title during that time: L.P.A. 1925, s.44 as amended by L.P.A. 1969, s.23.

(c) *imputed notice*: where a purchaser employs an agent, such as a solicitor, any notice (whether actual or constructive) attributed to the agent is imputed to the purchaser.

6. The protection of the doctrine of the bona fide purchaser for value of a legal estate with no notice of the equitable interest extends to any person claiming through such purchaser, even though they themselves may have notice of the equity: *Wilkes v. Spooner* (1911).

7. The impact and effect of the doctrine of notice has been considerably reduced by the property legislation of 1925 and the Land Charges Act 1972. Nevertheless the rule still applies in certain limited situations (see Chap. 5).

4. THE 1925 PROPERTY LEGISLATION

Introduction

1. A comprehensive and radical reform of property legislation was undertaken in 1925 because of the cumbersome method of conveying property and the survival of many anachronistic and outmoded rules and doctrines.

2. The legislation comprised:

(a) Law of Property Act;

(b) Settled Land Act;

(c) Trustee Act;

(d) Administration of Estates Act;

(e) Land Charges Act;

(f) Land Registration Act.

3. The legislation achieved the following general effects:

(a) reduced the number and effects of the tenure system;

(b) achieved closed approximation of land law and the law of personal property;

(c) reduced the number of legal estates in land;

(d) extended the system of registration of charges and registration of title;

(e) abrogated many miscellaneous outmoded rules.

4. There are now two separate systems of conveyancing in existence:

(a) unregistered conveyancing—where a purchaser of property requires a vendor to prove his title through production of the title deeds. A "root of title" of 15 years is currently required;

(b) registered conveyancing—this was introduced in 1925 and a purchaser checks title by reference to the Land Register (not to be confused with the Land Charges Register). Here the title to the property has been placed on a central register which is easy to check.

REDUCTION OF LEGAL ESTATES AND INTERESTS IN LAND—L.P.A. 1925, s.1

1. In an attempt to simplify conveyancing and assist a purchaser of property, one of the principal innovations of the L.P.A. 1925 was to reduce the number of legal estates in land. Section 1(1) of the Act provides that: "The only estates in land which are capable of subsisting or being conveyed or created at law are:

(a) an estate in fee simple absolute in possession;

(b) a term of years absolute."

The section further provides that there are five interests in or over land that are capable of being legal:

(a) an easement right or privilege in or over land equivalent to an estate in fee simple absolute in possession or a term of years absolute;

(b) a rentcharge in possession issued out of or charged on land being either perpetual or for a term of years absolute;

(c) a charge by way of legal mortgage;

(d) land taxes, tithe rentcharges and other similar charges (now abolished);

(e) rights of entry exercisable over or in respect of a legal term of years absolute, or annexed, for any purpose, to a legal rentcharge.

2. It follows that if an estate or interest is not contained in s.1 then it can only take effect as an equitable interest: L.P.A. 1925, s.1(2)(c). Examples would include entails and life estates.

3. An estate or interest in land is only capable of being legal if contained in section 1 *and* is created in the correct manner, *e.g.* by deed—s.52(1) L.P.A. 1925; s.1(2) L.P. (Miscellaneous Provisions) Act 1989. For example, an easement granted in writing could only be enforced in equity.

4. The difference between an "estate" and an "interest" is that an estate creates a right to possession, whereas an interest is a right over someone else's land.

LEGAL ESTATES

The fee simple absolute in possession

1. As has already been observed the fee simple is an estate of inheritance that lasts as long as the "owner" has heirs. The word "absolute" is used to distinguish a fee simple that may continue forever from a modified fee of which there are three main species:

(a) Determinable fee. A fee simple which may end on the happening of some contingency before its natural termination. Such a fee determines automatically if the contingent event ever occurs. Examples include; "to X in fee simple as long as the church tower on St Paul's never falls down" or "to X in fee simple until his bankruptcy."

(b) Fee simply on condition subsequent. A fee simple which determines on the occurrence of some event. If the event ever occurs the grantor has a right of re-entry but the estate does not automatically terminate. Examples include "to X in fee simple on condition that the church tower on St Paul's never falls down," or "to X in fee simple, but if he becomes bankrupt then to Y absolutely."

(c) Fee simple on condition precedent. A fee simple which will commence on a particular event, *e.g.* "to X and his heirs when he reaches the age of 30."

2. It is noticeable that there is a similarity between a determinable fee and a fee simple on condition subsequent. The difference is in the words used to connect the fee simple to the contingent event. Wherever the words set the limit for the estate first granted, it is determinable, *e.g.* "while," "during," or "as long as." Where the words form a grant subject to the possibility of it being defeated then a fee simple on condition subsequent is created, *e.g.* "on condition that," "if it happens that," "but if." The importance of the distinction is that whilst the determinable fee can only exist in equity behind a trust, (it not being "absolute" for the purposes of s.1) because of an anomaly in the law it is possible for a fee simple on condition subsequent to be "absolute." This stems from the wording of the Law Property Amendment Act 1926, which enacts in the context of rentcharges that "a fee simple subject to a legal or equitable right of entry or re-entry is for the purposes of this Act absolute." The provision was drafted so widely that it applies

to the fee simple on condition subsequent, even though this was not intended. Consequently, because a right of re-entry is given to a grantor, if the contingent event ever occurs under a fee simple on condition subsequent, this invokes the words of the Amendment Act and renders it a fee simple absolute.

3. If the condition attached to a determinable fee is rendered void (see below) then the whole grant fails, whereas if the estate is a conditional fee and the condition is rendered void, this creates a fee simple absolute and only the condition is affected. For this reason the courts are much stricter in construing conditional fees than they are in construing determinable fees based on the same type of condition. Conditions may be rendered void on the following grounds:

(a) vagueness: where precise definition cannot be given to the terms of the condition, *e.g. Re Jones* (1953)—a condition that the donee should not have a social or other relationship with a certain named person—void for uncertainty;

(b) prevents alienation: a provision which prevents the sale of the land may be void: *Hood v. Oglander* (1865), though a partial restraint may be valid: *Re Macleay* (1875);

(c) excluding bankruptcy: *Re Machu* (1882);

(d) restraint of marriage: *Clayton v. Ramsden* (1943), though a partial restraint may be valid. In *Re Tepper's Will Trusts* (1986) a reference to marrying outside "the Jewish faith" created uncertainty; however, extrinsic evidence as to the context of the statement was permitted to show its meaning.

(e) contrary to public policy; any provision that encourages immorality, illegality, the breakdown of marriage or the family will be inoperative.

4. A fee simple liable to divest or shift such as a grant of Blackacre "to A in fee simple, but if A becomes a solicitor then to B in fee simple" is subject to the statutory exception in L.P.A. 1925, s.7(1) which provides that a fee simple liable to be divested under the Land Clauses Acts or School Sites Acts or any similar statute is considered absolute even though it may still divest: *Re Rowhook* (1984). Under section 7(2) a fee simple vested in a corporate body is still absolute although it may determine on dissolution.

5. A fee simple will be absolute even if incumbered, whether by mortgage, restrictive covenant or otherwise.

6. The term "in possession" in section 1(1)(a) is used to distinguish present enjoyment from enjoyment in the future. A grant to "A for life; remainder to B in fee simple" does not give B a legal estate. Possession includes receipt of rent and profits of land, or

the right to receive them: L.P.A., s.205(1)(XIX). A fee simple owner who has leased his land is still a legal estate owner even if he does not have physical possession.

A term of years absolute

1. This is a legal estate of fixed duration and includes, in accordance with L.P.A. 1925, s.205(1)(XXVII), a term of less than a year, or for a year or years or a fraction of a year, or from year to year. In effect any period with a fixed minimum duration which includes a periodic tenancy.

2. The term absolute appears to have little meaning though the L.P.A., s.205 provides that a term of years will still be absolute even though it may be liable to determination by notice, re-entry, operation of law, or by a provision for cesser on redemption (of mortgage) or on any other event. A lease which ceases on the dropping of a life is not absolute.

3. There is no requirement that the lease should be in possession; it may commence in the future (although L.P.A. 1925, s.149 makes most reversionary leases void if they are to take effect more than 21 years from the date of the instrument of creation).

Legal interests—L.P.A. 1925, s.1(2)

1. Easements rights and privileges. The definition will extend to cover *profits à prendre* but not restrictive covenants. The grant must be perpetual or for a fixed term, so that a grant of an easement for life is necessarily equitable, such easement being registrable if created after 1925.

2. Rentcharges. A rentcharge is a right to a periodical sum of money secured on land:

    (a) the definition requires the rentcharge to be "in possession" which appears to mean that it must not commence in the future from the time it was granted. This has been negated by the terms of the L.P. (Entailed Interests) Act 1932, which permits future rentcharges except those that are in remainder: See now Rentcharges Act 1977;

    (b) the rentcharge must be issued out of or charged on land, which covers the situation where a rentcharge is issued out of an already existing rentcharge;

    (c) the period of the rentcharge must be fixed or perpetual.

This definition must now be read in the light of the Rentcharges Act 1977 which provides:

    (a) no new rentcharge can be created after the coming into force of the Act (August 1977). "Estate rentcharges" provide an exception to this;

(b) existing rentcharges are to have a maximum life of 60 years calculated from the date of commencement of the rent-charge or the date the Act comes into force, whichever is the later.

3. Charge by way of legal mortgage. This is an example of one of the two ways of creating a legal mortgage after 1925, the other being the grant of a term of years absolute.

4. Land tax. . . . No longer of importance.

5. Rights of entry. If a tenant under a legal lease fails to pay rent or comply with other covenants in the lease, the landlord has a right to re-enter, that right being a legal interest. Similarly, if a legal rentcharge falls into arrear the grantee has a legal right to enter to collect his money.

6. Any former estate or interest not falling within the above headings may nevertheless be enforceable as equitable interests.

EXTENSION OF THE SYSTEM OF REGISTRATION OF LAND CHARGES

1. A system of registration of certain equitable interests was possible before 1926, though this was extended substantially by the 1925 legislation particularly in respect of those rights that were unsuited to the overreaching mechanism. "Commercial" interests, as distinct from "family" interests, were in the main given the protection of registration whereas "family" interests, such as those arising under a settlement were protected by the overreaching machinery.

2. The system of registration of land charges has to a great extent replaced the doctrine of notice in respect of third party rights. This form of registration should not be confused with "registration of title" which is a form of conveyancing where title to property, instead of being traced through the title deeds, is discovered through a register of title which contains all the relevant details relating to the land.

Principles of registration

1. After 1925 whether an equitable interest binds a purchaser depends not on whether he has notice of it, but whether or not that interest has been registered (provided it is registrable). This is a substantial improvement from the point of view of practical convenience.

2. Registration of a registrable right is deemed to constitute actual notice to all persons and for all purposes connected with the land: L.P.A. 1925, s.198. Failure to register makes the interest void against a purchaser: L.C.A. 1972, s.4. Where the registrable interest is an estate contract; restrictive covenant (post 1926); equitable easement or a charge for death duties and the interest has not been registered it is void against a purchaser of a legal estate "for money or money's worth." All other registrable interests are void against a purchaser "for value." In *Lloyds Bank v. Carrick* (1996) an unregistered C(iv) was held void for lack of registration. Whether a purchaser has actual notice or not in these situations is irrelevant: *Hollingworth Bros v. Rhodes* (1931): L.P.A. 1925, s.199(1)(i). Even if an equitable interest is registrable and has not been registered, it will still bind individuals who are not purchasers and therefore not protected by the Act, *e.g.* a person who takes as a gift.

3. Registration of incumbrances is now governed by the Land Charges Act 1972 (replacing L.C.A. 1925) and in order for a purchaser to obtain quick discovery of third party equitable rights (which are registrable) a search in the land charges register provides this.

4. Land charges are registered against the name of the estate owner, not against the land: *Oak Co-operative Building Society v. Blackburn* (1968). Since the coming into force of the Law of Property (Miscellaneous Provisions) Act 1994, s.15, on July 1, 1995, a landcharge can be registered against an estate owner after his death whereas previously this was not possible.

Mechanics of registration

1. There are five registers created under the Land Charges Act 1972, s.1(1) all kept in the land charges department of the Land Registry at Plymouth:

    (a) register of pending actions;
    (b) register of annuities;
    (c) register of writs and orders affecting land;
    (d) register of deeds of arrangement;
    (e) land charges register.

It is the land charges register that is of principal concern. Within the register there are six classifications, though only class C, D and F require significant attention.

2. Class C landcharges

    (a) a puisne mortgage: a legal mortgage not protected by deposit of title deeds. Registration of such a *legal* right is to preserve priority of the mortgage;

(b) a limited owner's charge: a charge on land by a person who is not an absolute owner, *e.g.* a tenant for life who pays inheritance tax out of his own pocket may secure payment by such a charge;

(c) a general equitable charge: A residuary class which covers equitable charges that are not registrable elsewhere. In essence any equitable charge that affects the legal estate, *e.g.* an equitable rentcharge, or an equitable mortgage of a legal estate;

(d) an estate contract: a contract by an estate owner to convey or create a legal estate. The contract must amount to a binding and enforceable agreement: *Mens v. Wilson* (1973). The definition covers ordinary contracts for sale, leasing or mortgaging of the legal estate, as well as a right of pre-emption (first refusal) and an option to purchase: *Midland Bank v. Green* (1980)—an option to purchase not registered was void against a purchaser of a legal estate for money or money's worth. In *Phillips v. Mobil Oil Co. Ltd* (1989), an option to renew contained in a lease, being an estate contract, was void as against a purchaser for money or money's worth of a legal estate, for want of registration. Options to dispose of an interest in land must now comply with s.2, L.P. (Miscellaneous Provisions) Act 1989: *Spiro v. Glencrown Properties Ltd* (1991). A request for an overriding lease under the Landlord and Tenant (Covenants) Act 1995, s.20(6) may be registered under the Land Charges Act 1972 as if it were an estate contract.

3. Class D landcharges

(a) a charge for unpaid inheritance tax in favour of the Inland Revenue;

(b) restrictive covenants: any covenant that restricts user of land can be registered provided it was entered into after 1925 and was not made between a landlord and tenant. Restrictive covenants made prior to 1926 still depend on the doctrine of notice;

(c) equitable easements: created after 1925 and being equivalent to the definition in L.P.A. 1925, s.1(2)(*a*); *Shiloh Spinners v. Harding* (1973). Certain easements in equity are not covered by the definition and are not registrable: *Ives v. High* (1967)—easement acquired by acquiescence or estoppel.

4. Class F landcharges The right of a spouse who does not hold the legal estate in the matrimonial home to occupy the matrimonial home under the Matrimonial Homes Act 1983. If, for example, a husband holds the legal estate as sole owner or on trust for himself and his spouse by way of co-ownership, the spouse will have the right to register a charge and protect her rights of occupation.

(a) the right of occupation cannot be taken away without the leave of the court: s.1(1);

(b) successors in title are bound by these rights of occupation where the owning spouse's rights are based on an estate or interest, as distinct from a contract or statute: *Wroth v. Tyler* (1974);

(c) the Class F landcharge can be set aside where misused: *Barnett v. Hassett* (1981).

Once the provisions of the Family Law Act 1996 are fully brought into force the spouse's rights of occupation of the matrimonial home and other rights relating to matrimonial property will be replaced by new "matrimonial home rights" which will be registrable under the Land Registration Act 1925 as a notice, or as a Class F charge under the Land Charges Act 1972 where title is unregistered.

Equitable interests that are not registrable or overreachable

In general, family equitable interests in unregistered land are protected under the overreaching machinery, whereas commercial equitable interests are protected by registration as land charges. Certain equitable interests are not registrable within the terms of the Land Charges Act 1972. Provided they are not within the species of interest that are overreachable, whether they bind a purchaser or not is determined by the doctrine of notice. Such interests include:

(a) restrictive covenants created before 1926;

(b) equitable easements created before 1926;

(c) beneficial interests under a bare trust;

(d) pre-1926 equitable mortgages where there is a deposit of title deeds or there has been no transfer since 1925;

(e) equitable rights of entry;

(f) equitable rights based on acquiescence or estoppel; *Ives v. High* (1967);

(g) beneficial interests arising under resulting trusts or by way of a contractual licence.

Overreaching

1. Successive interests in land were created after 1925 by way of a strict settlement under the Settled Land Act 1925 or by way of a trust for sale under the Law of Property Act 1925. With both mechanisms the legal estate and beneficial interests were often divorced. In such situations two problems arose:

(a) how could the land be made easily sellable without the purchaser being inconvenienced by the interests of the beneficiaries; and

(b) how could the interests of the beneficiaries be protected?

2. The interests of the beneficiaries under a settlement or a trust for sale were not registrable so as to give notice to a purchaser from trustees. The problem was solved by the overreaching machinery introduced under the 1925 legislation. This was a mechanism which provided that a beneficiary's interest did not bind a purchaser of the land where the purchaser paid the purchase money to at least two trustees or a trust corporation. The interest of the beneficiary was not extinguished, it was transferred to the purchase money which had taken its place and was in the hands of the trustees, who had to safeguard it on penalty of breach of trust.

3. The overreaching principle did not affect interests that were registrable under the Land Charges Act 1972.

4. As to the effects of the overreaching principle; *Williams & Glyn's Bank v. Boland* (1981), a wife's equitable interest in land was not overreachable by a subsequent mortgage (Bank acting as mortgagees). Contrast *City of London Building Society v. Flegg* (1988): family arrangement, where the interests in a family property were shared by parents and their adult children. Here, the legal estate being in the hands of the adult children was mortgaged by them to a building society. It was held that the interests of the parents were overreached, their interests having been switched to the proceeds of sale on the creation of the mortgage.

5. Under the Trusts of Land and Appointment of Trustees Act 1996 extensive changes to the way successive interests in land are created have taken place (see Chap. 6). Most significant is the abolition of the trust for sale and the doctrine of conversion, the barring of the creation of any new strict settlements and the replacement of the old system with a new trust of land. The overreaching mechanism is retained so that if, for example, a purchaser buy lands subject to co-ownership from at least two trustees, then the interests of the beneficiaries are overreached and transferred to the purchase money. New consultation provisions that require trustees to give effect to the wishes of the beneficiaries, so far as

is consistent with the purposes of the trust of land, ought to reduce though not eradicate the number of situations where overreaching will occur (see ss. 10, 11, 14 of the 1996 Act). Where the purchase money is paid to only one trustee for sale the overreaching mechanisms cannot operate and the purchaser will be bound by rights of the beneficial owners.

5. LEASES

Introduction

1. A lease is an estate in land of defined duration. It is capable of being a legal estate under L.P.A. 1925, s.1(1)(*b*) provided it is a "term of years absolute" defined in L.P.A. 1925, s.205(1)(XXVII) and as long as it is created in the correct manner, as specified in L.P.A. 1925, ss. 52 and 54.

2. The terms lease, term of years, demise and tenancy are often used interchangeably, though a tenancy is normally of shorter duration. The landlord is often referred to as the grantor or lessor and the tenant as the grantee or lessee. The landlord on granting a lease retains a reversion which is essential to the landlord and tenant relationship. Either the leasehold term or the landlord's reversion may be assigned (*i.e.* transferred) and the tenant may grant a sublease (under-lease) for any period at least one day shorter than the period which he himself holds.

UNUSUAL LEASES

Perpetually renewable leases

1. A lease in perpetuity is void as it does not constitute a "term of years absolute"; however, a perpetually renewable lease, *i.e.* one where the power of renewal is given as often as the lease expires, may be valid. By virtue of L.P.A. 1922, s.145 and 15th Schedule, such leases are converted into terms of 2000 years.

2. Perpetually renewable leases are created by giving, as in *Caerphilly Concrete Products Ltd v. Owen* (1972), the right to renew "on the same terms and conditions including this clause" or as in *Northchurch Estate v. Daniels* (1947), by granting a renewal "on identical terms and conditions." In *Marjorie Burnett v. Barclay* (1980), the court expressed the view that it leant against the creation of per-

petually renewable leases unless there was an express reference to
the covenant for renewal included in the lease.

3. Special incidents attach to perpetually renewable leases:

    (a) only the tenant can terminate the lease, on what would have
been a renewal date, by giving 10 days' notice;

    (b) any assignment or devolution must be notified to the land-
lord within six months;

    (c) on any assignment, the original tenant is not liable for
breaches of covenant committed after the assignment;

    (d) any fine or other payment on renewal for which the lease
provides is void if the lease is made after 1925. In pre-1926
leases the sum is converted into extra rent and spread over
the period.

4. An option to renew a lease for over 60 years is void, but this
only applies to single renewals and not perpetually renewable
leases; L.P.A. 1922, Schedule 15, para. 7.

Leases for life

1. Under L.P.A. 1925, s.149(6) a lease at a rent or fine, for life
or lives, or for any term of years determinable with life or lives or
on the marriage of the lessee is converted into a 90-year-lease,
whether or not granted before or after 1925. The section would
incorporate;

    (a) a lease to X for life;

    (b) a lease to X for 10 years if he so long lives;

    (c) a lease to X for 99 years if he so long remains a bachelor.

2. For the section to be invoked the lease must be at a rent or
fine and consequently does not apply to gratuitous leases.

3. Any lease within the section does not terminate on death or
marriage (whichever the case may be). On such an event either
party may determine by giving the other party (or heir) at least
one month's written notice to expire on one of the quarter days.

4. A lease where no rent or fine is given may fall within the
ambit of the Settled Land Act 1925 and create a strict settlement:
s.20(1)(iv); *Binions v. Evans* (1972); *Ungurian v. Lesnoff* (1989).

5. An example of the effects of s.149(6) LPA is provided by the
decision in *Skipton Building Society v. Clayton* (1993). Here, the rent-
free nature of a term of years was brought within s.149(6) in order
for it "to take effect as a lease . . . for a term of 90 years".

THE ESSENTIALS OF A LEASE

Provided a lease has been created by using the correct formalities
a term of years absolute will be valid if two pre-requisites have
been satisfied:

(a) exclusive possession;
(b) certainty of duration.

Exclusive possession

1. The right to exclusive possession is the right to exclude all others from the premises including the landlord. If such right is not conferred upon the grantee then it is likely that he hold merely a licence, which is a personal revocable interest which does not have the protections given by the Rent Act 1977 (controlled rents and security of tenure): Housing Act 1988.

2. If the grantor remains in general control of the property (as with an inn or a boarding house) a licence is likely to be inferred: *Wells v. Kingston upon Hull Corp.* (1875)—a graving dock was "let" but the Corporation retained the right to open and shut gates and clean the docks. It was held that only a licence and not a lease had been created because general control remained with the Corporation: *Manchester C.C. v. N.C.P. Ltd* (1982). A lodger does not enjoy exclusive possession: *A.G. Securities v. Vaughan* (1988); *Antoniades v. Villiers* (1988). Where a landlord retains a key to the premises this does not of itself negative exclusive possession: *Family Housing Association v. Jones* (1990).

3. The granting of exclusive possession is essential to the creation of a lease, though if it is granted it does not automatically follow that the grantee is a tenant, *i.e.* it is necessary but not sufficient. Until recently, in construing any agreement the intention of the parties as inferred from the agreement and surrounding circumstances was the test applied by the courts in determining whether a licence or a lease had been created: *Somma v. Hazelhurst* (1978). In 1985 a fundamental review of the law was undertaken by the House of Lords in *Street v. Mountford*. It is no longer the intention of the parties that is essential but the court's construction of the agreement and in examining such agreement the presence or absence of exclusive possession is of critical importance: *Bretherton v. Paton* (1986). Where the attempt to exclude exclusive possession is a sham it will not be recognised: *Antoniades v. Villiers* (1988). All surrounding circumstances must be taken into account: *Stibling v. Wickham* (1989). The courts will consider whether the terms of the agreement were part of the true bargain made between the parties or merely a pretence and therefore to be ignored: *Aslan v. Murphy* (1989).

4. In exceptional circumstances, even where exclusive possession exists, a licence may be inferred rather than a tenancy.

(a) Family arrangements—as in *Cobb v. Lane* (1952) and *Hard-*

wicke v. Johnson (1978). However, the existence of a family relationship does not always prevent a tenancy as can be seen from *Nunn v. Dalyrymple* (1990) and *Ward v. Wanke* (1990). Each situation depends upon the intention of the parties and the inferences to be drawn from the circumstances.

(b) Acts of Friendship or Charity: *Booker v. Palmer* (1942).

(c) Employees: a distinction has to be drawn between where a person is genuinely required to occupy the premises for the better performance of his duties and where a person occupies as a fringe benefit or an inducement to encourage the employee to work better: *Norris v. Checksfield* (1991).

5. The position since *Street v. Mountford* (1985), would seem to be:

(a) in cases where exclusive possession exists, but the relationship of the parties negates a tenancy, then a licence is created: *Monmouth B.C. v. Marlog* (1994);

(b) where there are no exceptional facts, if exclusive possession exists the inference of a tenancy becomes almost irresistible: *Nicolaou v. Pitt* (1989).

6. The basic test of exclusive possession is applicable to commercial premises: *London & Associated Trust v. Calow* (1986).

7. Where a landlord does not have the power to grant tenancies then the agreement may constitute a licence: *Camden London Borough Council v. Shortlife Community Housing Ltd* (1992).

Certainty of duration

1. In general, a lease must have a certain beginning and a certain ending, though the parties may stipulate that a lease is to commence on the happening of an uncertain event, *e.g.* on possession being obtained from a previous tenant. Where it is impossible to quantify the duration of the term the lease is void: *Lace v. Chantler* (1944), a lease for the duration of the war would have been void but for the provisions of the Validation of Wartime Leases Act 1944, which converted such leases into terms of 10 years. A lease for the "duration of Parliament" would be invalid. Recently a lease to continue "until the landlord requires the land for road widening purposes" was held to be invalid for uncertainty: *Prudential Assurance Co. Ltd v. London Residuary Body* (1992), as was a lease to continue "so long as the company is trading": *Birrel v. Carey* (1989). Similarly the commencement date of the lease must be certain. In *Askew v. Tarmac Roadstone Holdings* (1991) a lease containing a commencement date by reference to the date of a planning permission at some future date was held to be too uncertain.

2. A term of years absolute does not have to be "in possession," so that reversionary leases are permissible, save where they conflict with the terms of L.P.A. 1925, s.149(3). This provides that a lease at a rent or fine to take effect more than 21 years from the date of the instrument creating it is void. A contract to create such a term is similarly void. The section does not apply to leases created prior to 1926, nor to leases in equity, nor to a tenant's option for renewal: *Re Strand and Savoy Properties Ltd* (1960).

Rent

The rent payable under a lease must be certain. Despite the fact that L.P.A. 1925, s.205(1)(XXVII) defines a term of years as "taking effect in possession or in reversion *whether or not at a rent*" there has been some dispute as to whether payment of rent is an essential of a lease. Lord Templeman in *Street v. Mountford* (1985) suggested that it was necessary and support for this can be found in *Morris v. Carey* (1989). However, the better view seems to be that the reservation of rent is not essential for the creation of a lease: *Skipton Building Society v. Clayton* (1993).

FORMALITIES FOR THE CREATION OF A LEASE

Legal leases

1. Post 1925 the creation of legal leases is governed by L.P.A. 1925, ss. 52 and 54. A legal lease for any period greater than three years can only be created by deed: s.52(1). No deed or writing is required at law for a lease taking effect in possession, for a term not exceeding three years (whether or not the lessee is given the power to extend the term); at the best rent reasonably obtainable without taking a fine: s.54(1). The term "possession" includes receipt of rent and profits from a sub-tenant: L.P.A., s.205. The definition also incorporated periodic tenancies. In *Long v. Tower Hamlets* (1996) a letter confirming a tenancy to commence three weeks later was not a lease taking effect in possession under s.54(2).

2. A deed is required for any assignment of a legal lease, even one which has been created orally under the three-year exception: *Crago v. Julian* (1992).

Leases enforceable in equity

1. Before the coming into effect of the Law of Property (Miscellaneous Provisions) Act 1989 on September 27, 1989 if a lease was void at law it could still be valid in equity provided:

(a) it was for valuable consideration; and

(b) it complied with L.P.A. 1925, s.40(1) or was evidenced by an act of part performance.

Equity treated an unenforceable legal lease as a contract to create a lease and at its discretion granted specific performance of its terms.

2. Under L.P.A., s.40(1) it was provided that:

> "No action may be brought upon any contract for the sale, or other disposition of land or any interest in land, unless the agreement upon which such action is brought, or some memorandum or note thereof, is in writing and signed by the party to be charged or by some other person thereunto by him lawfully authorised."

The section required written evidence of the contract, not necessarily a complete written contract. The evidence had to extend to at least: parties; premises; duration of the lease, rent or other consideration and date of commencement, together with every other material term. Evidence need not have been in any particular form and joinder of documents was possible: *Elias v. Sahely* (1982). Section 40 did not make a contract outside its terms void, but merely unenforceable by action. It was still a valid contract for other purposes (*e.g.* as to deposit).

3. The Law of Property (Miscellaneous Provisions) Act 1989 has now repealed section 40 of L.P.A. 1925 and has replaced it with the following section: section 2(1) a contract for the sale or other disposition of an interest in land can only be made in writing and only by incorporating all the terms which the parties have expressly agreed in one document or, where contracts are exchanged, in each.

(a) The new provision only applies to agreements entered into after September 27, 1989. Section 40 still applies to agreements entered into before that date, as was illustrated recently in *Lloyds Bank v. Carrick* (1996).

(b) Section 2 does not apply to short leases, *i.e.* leases for not more than three years at the best rent reasonably obtainable without taking a fine: L.P.A., s.54(2).

(c) Section 2 requires the agreement to be *in writing* not merely *evidenced in writing*. In relation to options, see *Spiro v. Glencrown Properties Ltd* (1991).

(d) Under section 2 *both* parties must sign the agreement whereas under section 40 only "the party to be charged" was required to do so. The decision in *First Homes Ltd v. Johnson* (1995) examined the requirement of the signature, a letter containing the terms of the contract was signed by the vendor while an accompanying plan was signed by the vendor and an agent for the purchaser. The Court of Appeal held that the letter and the plan did not constitute a single document as required by s.2.

(e) The statute requires all terms of the agreement to be on one document (except exchange of contracts). This, however, does not apply to supplemental agreements which are separate to and distinct from the main agreement (lease) itself: *Tootal Clothing Ltd v. Guinea Properties Management Ltd* (1992). The courts will construe the agreements strictly and will not find separate contracts where in reality there is only one contract, but with two elements: *Wright v. Robert Leonard (Developments) Ltd* (1994); *McCausland v. Duncan Lawrie* (1996).

The extent of the operation of s.2 of the 1989 Act has been the subject of considerable recent litigation which has determined:

(a) an option to surrender a lease was within the terms of the section: *Commission for the New Towns v. Cooper (Great Britain) Ltd* (1995);

(b) an exchange of letters might satisfy the terms of s.2: *Hooper v. Sherman* (1994), though doubt was raised on this in *Commission for the New Towns v. Cooper (Great Britain) Ltd* (1995);

(c) s.2 will apply to variations of a contract: *McCausland v. Duncan Lawrie* (1996);

(d) a valid equitable charge by deposit of the land certificate requires a written mortgage agreement satisfying s.2: *United Bank of Kuwait v. Sahib* (1996).

4. It is important to remember that section 40 of L.P.A. may still apply in certain situations. If a contract is unenforceable under section 40(1) it is uncertain as to whether the equitable doctrine of part performance can still apply. Although not expressly abolished by the 1989 Act the better view is that part performance will not apply as the effect of section 2 of the 1989 Act renders the contract a nullity not merely unenforceable and therefore part performance has no operation. This was the view of Gibson L.J. in *Firstpost Homes Ltd v. Johnson* (1995), though a contrary view was expressed by Neill L.J. in *Singh v. Beggs* (1996). If part performance is still to apply it must be established that the person seeking to enforce the contract has carried out some act which on the balance of probabilities was carried out because a contract was in existence. In *Steadman v. Steadman* (1974), the test of "unequivocal referability" was rejected in favour of the "balance of probabilities" test.

5. The effect of part performance was to allow evidence of all the

terms of the contract, but only equitable remedies were available.

6. It may be argued that part performance should be permitted on the basis that "equity will not allow a statute to be used as an engine of fraud". If evidence of fraud exists equity may still step in to enforce the contract. A further possibility would be to view the situation in the context of estoppel.

7. Whilst equity treats an imperfect (unenforceable) legal lease as a contract to which equity may grant specific performance, an agreement for a lease which complies with section 2, 1989 Act is similarly treated so that the remedy may equally be available. Before an agreement can be enforced final and complete agreement must have been reached, *i.e.* the parties are beyond the stage of negotiations. An agreement "subject to contract" is not enforceable: *Regalian Properties v. London Dockland Development Corporation* (1994), though a provisional agreement until a fully legalised agreement is signed is binding: *Branca v. Cobarro* (1947).

8. The rule in *Walsh v. Lonsdale* (1882): in equity specific performance may be granted of an imperfect lease which is treated as a contract. Once it has been granted the parties are in the position of having a lease by deed. Before it is granted but when the parties are entitled to ask for it, "equity looks on that as done which ought to be done" and all terms of the agreement are enforceable as if it was a legal lease. This maxim is reflected in the often cited statement that "an agreement for a lease is as good as a legal lease." See also *Industrial Properties v. A.E.I.* (1977).

9. An agreement for a lease is not as good as a legal lease for the following reasons:

(a) a contract is dependent on specific performance which is a discretionary remedy and may not be granted if, for example, a tenant is in breach of his obligation: *Coatsworth v. Johnson* (1886); *Sudbrook Trading Estate Ltd v. Eggleton* (1982);

(b) a legal lease creates an estate enforceable against all third parties, whereas a contract is not enforceable against certain purchasers of a legal estate. An agreement is an estate contract which, if created after 1925, is registrable as a land charge. If it is not registered it is void against a purchaser of a legal estate for money or money's worth. In a registered land situation an estate contract is a minor interest which should be protected by entry on the register by virtue of a notice or caution. Protection may also arise under the Land Registration Act 1925, s.70(1)(g) if the holder is in actual occupation of the property.

(c) the burden of certain covenants does not pass on an assignment of an agreement for a lease;
(d) a contract is not a "conveyance" for the purpose of L.P.A. 1925, s.62;
(e) the holder of an agreement can never claim to be a bona fide purchaser for value of a *legal estate* with no notice of an equitable interest.

Tenancies

1. Periodic tenancy. Apart from express agreement a periodic tenancy may arise whenever a person goes into possession with the owner's consent and pays rent by reference to a definite period, *e.g.* weekly, monthly, quarterly, yearly. Such tenancy is a legal term of years absolute under L.P.A., s.54(2). The parties to the tenancy may specifically agree to a period of notice determining the tenancy, but in the absence of this the following periods of notice must be given:
(a) yearly tenancy—two quarters if the tenancy began on a quarterday, otherwise six calendar months;
(b) quarterly—one quarter's notice;
(c) monthly—one month's notice.
Under the Protection from Eviction Act 1977, no notice to quit any premises let as a dwelling shall be valid unless in writing and given four weeks before the date it is to become effective.

2. Tenancy at will. Where a tenant is let into possession at the will of the landlord, who may determine the tenancy whenever he wishes, a tenancy at will is created. If rent is later paid it is converted into a periodic tenancy. A tenancy at will may be expressly created: *Cardiothoracic Institute v. Shrewdcrest* (1986); *Javad v. Aqil* (1991).

3. Tenancy at sufferance. Where a tenant holds over after his lease has expired and remains in possession, a tenancy at sufferance is created. The tenant may be liable for double rent (yearly value of the land) and the landlord can claim possession at any time.

4. Tenancy by estoppel. This arises where a landlord purports to grant a lease at a time when he holds no estate in the land. If the landlord later acquires the legal estate he is estopped from denying the tenancy. This "feeds the estoppel."

THE RIGHTS AND DUTIES OF LANDLORD AND TENANT

The rights and duties of the parties to the lease are normally determined by the provisions of the lease itself. Where the lease is silent certain covenants are implied by common law and statute.

Implied obligations of the landlord

1. Covenant for quiet enjoyment. The tenant has a right to be put into possession at the commencement of the term and is entitled to damages if his enjoyment is substantially interfered with by acts of the landlord. Examples usually take the form of direct physical interference such as the cutting off of gas or electricity: *cf. Browne v. Flower* (1911); *Owen v. Gadd* (1956). As to rights created via title paramount: *Celsteel Limited v. Alton House Holdings Limited (No. 2)* (1987). Insulting and violent behaviour may amount to a breach: *Sampson v. Floyd* (1989). Compensation for injured feelings and mental distress cannot be given as damages for breach, although damages can be recovered in tort for trespass and exemplary damages may be recovered in tort in appropriate cases: *Branchett v. Bleaney* (1992).

2. Not to derogate from the grant. The landlord must not frustrate the use of the land for the purpose for which it was let. For example if a flat is leased for residential purposes, and the remainder of the building was obviously intended for similar purposes, that remainder may not be let for business purposes: *Newman v. Real Estate Debentures Corp.* (1940).

3. Repair and fitness for habitation. There is no general implied undertaking at common law that the landlord guarantees that premises are fit for habitation, or for any particular purpose or even that they are not dangerous. Nevertheless certain exceptions should be noted:

(a) furnished dwelling-houses—must be reasonably fit for human habitation when let: *Smith v. Marrable* (1843)—bug-infested premises;

(b) houses let at a low rent under the Landlord and Tenant Act 1985, ss.8–10, implied condition that the landlord will keep premises fit for human habitation throughout the tenancy;

(c) lettings of a dwelling-house for less than seven years under the Landlord and Tenant Act 1985, ss. 11–16 as amended: the landlord must keep in repair the structure and exterior of the dwelling house, including drains, pipes and gutters and also keep in repair and proper working order the installations in the house for water, gas, electricity, sanitation and space and water heating: *Quick v. Taff Ely B.C.* (1985); *McClean v. Liverpool City Council* (1987); *Post Office v. Aquarius Properties Ltd* (1986). In *Staves & Staves v. Leeds C.C.* (1991) it was held that dampness in plasterwork was part of the structure and exterior and the landlord was liable (even though the saturation of the plasterwork resulted from an inherent defect). However, a landlord may not be liable for inherent defects if their remedy would amount to improvements to the property;

(d) blocks of flats: if a landlord retains control of the means of access such as lifts and staircases, then he is under an obligation to keep them in repair: *Liverpool Corp. v. Irwin* (1977);

(e) defective premises: under the Defective Premises Act 1972, s.4, the landlord is under an obligation to take reasonable care to ensure that persons who might be affected by defects in the premises are reasonably safe from injury or damage: *McAuley v. Bristol City Council* (1991); *Targett v. Torfaen B.C.* (1992).

Implied obligations and rights of a tenant

1. To repair: a tenant must keep and deliver up the premises in a tenant-like manner. Such obligation may arise under the doctrine of waste: *Warren v. Kean* (1954).

2. To pay rent.

3. To pay rates and taxes.

4. To allow the landlord to view the premises if he is liable to repair.

5. A tenant has the implied right to emblements (to reap what he has sown); estovers (the right to take wood from the land); and the right to certain fixtures.

Usual covenants

1. Under a contract for a lease, a term is implied that the "usual covenants" shall be in the lease. A covenant by the landlord for quiet enjoyment is implied as are the following covenants by the tenant:

(a) to pay rent;
(b) to pay tenant's rates and taxes;
(c) to keep and deliver up in repair;
(d) to permit the landlord to view if he is obliged to repair;

(e) a condition for re-entry on non-payment of rent.

2. The category of usual covenants is not closed: *Flexman v. Corbett* (1930). Evidence of what is usual in a particular district for that type of property is usually taken: *Chester v. Buckingham Travel* (1981).

Express covenants and conditions

Most leases contain express provisions which determine the rights and liabilities of the parties. The covenants are varied and numerous though most commonly the landlord covenants to give quiet enjoyment and often to keep the property in repair, whilst the tenant usually agrees to pay rent and rates, not to assign without the landlord's consent, to insure and to repair the property.

Covenants to repair. 1. The wording of a covenant to repair often varies, *e.g.* "good tenantable repair"; "substantial repair"; "perfect repair." Generally the wording used adds nothing to the word "repair": *Proudfoot v. Hart* (1890); each implies such repair as, having regard to the age, character and locality of the house would make it reasonably fit for the occupation of a reasonably minded tenant of the class who were likely to take it. Particularly with old buildings renewal of subsidiary parts may be involved in "repair" but not complete reconstruction: *Brew Bros v. Snax* (1970). Any covenant is construed as at the commencement of the lease. As to whether building works constitute more than repair, see the tests laid down in *McDougal v. Easington D.C.* (1989). A covenant which required the landlord to keep the building in "good and tenantable condition" was wide enough to require him to put it into that condition even if it had never been so tenantable: *Crédit Suisse v. Beegas Nominees Ltd* (1994). The general rule that a covenant to keep premises in repair obliged the covenantor to keep them in repair at all times, so that he is in breach immediately a defect occurs, is subject to an exception that where the obligation is the landlord's the breach will only occur when the landlord has information about the repair and has failed to carry out remedial work within a reasonable time: *British Telecommunications v. Sun Life Assurance Society* (1995).

2. The covenant to repair may contain an exception for "fair wear and tear" which exonerates the covenantor from disrepair for normal human use and normal action of the elements. However, the covenantor is bound to do such repairs as may be required to prevent the consequences flowing originally from wear and tear from producing others which wear and tear would not directly pro-

duce: *Haskell v. Marlow* (1928); *Regis Property Co. Ltd v. Dudley* (1959).

3. The normal remedy for breach of a covenant to repair is damages, though in exceptional cases specific performance may be granted. *Jeune v. Queens Cross Properties Ltd* (1974). In terms of damages, the quantum cannot exceed the diminution in the value of the reversion, and no damages can be recovered where the premises are to be demolished or structurally altered so as to make repairs valueless at or soon after the end of the term: Landlord and Tenant Act 1927, s.18(1). A claim for the cost of alternative accommodation whilst the premises are uninhabitable is permissible: *Calabar v. Stitcher* (1984).

Covenant against assigning sub-letting or parting with possession. 1. In the absence of any express provision in a lease a tenant may transfer the property freely by way of assignment, sub-lease or otherwise. Any express provision in the lease will be strictly construed: *Marks v. Warren* (1979). In *Field v. Barkworth* (1986) a covenant not to assign or underlet *any part* of the premises was broken by an assignment of the whole. In general a covenant should prohibit assignment, underletting and parting with possession of the whole or any part or parts.

2. The form of the covenant may be absolute or qualified:
(a) absolute: creates a prohibition which is enforceable in its terms though it may be waived by the landlord;
(b) qualified: prohibits assignment ... "without the consent of the landlord". The Landlord and Tenant Act 1927, s.19(1)(a) adds the proviso that such consent cannot be unreasonably withheld.

3. A tenant must actually request consent before he can take advantage of section 19(1), if not he is *ipso facto* in breach of covenant.

4. The question of "reasonableness" was reviewed recently by the Court of Appeal in *International Drilling Fluids Ltd v. Louisville Investments (Uxbridge) Ltd* (1985), where the court specified:
(a) in each case, it is a question of fact, depending upon all the circumstances, whether the landlord's consent to an assignment is being unreasonably withheld: *Bickel v. Duke of Westminster* (1977);
(b) the test is objective: *Pimms v. Tallow Chandlers Co.* (1964);
(c) the landlord's refusal will normally be classed as unreasonable unless based on the character of the assignee ... or proposed use of the premises: *Houlder Bros. & Co. v. Gibbs* (1925);

(d) there is divergence of authority on the question of whether, in considering the landlord's refusal, it is permissible to have regard to the consequences to the tenant if consent is refused: *West Layton Ltd v. Ford* (1979); *Leeward Securities Ltd v. Lilyheath Properties Ltd* (1983).

5. Under the Landlord and Tenant act 1988, s.1(1) a statutory duty is imposed upon a landlord to make a decision, once his consent is requested, within a reasonable time of the tenant's application. This is provided the covenant is qualified in nature. If the landlord's consent is sought in writing the burden of proof is shifted to the landlord to show that he has not refused his consent unreasonably. If the landlord is deemed to have unreasonably refused, he commits a tort which will entitle the tenant to obtain damages or an injunction. In respect of assured tenancies: the Housing Act 1988, s.15 will apply and section 19(1) of the Landlord and Tenant Act 1927 is expressly excluded.

6. Under the Race Relations Act 1976, s.24 it is unreasonable to withhold consent to an assignment if based upon colour, race, nationality or ethnic or national origins, though the section does not apply where:

(a) the person withholding consent, or a near relative of his, resides and intends to continue to reside on the premises; and

(b) such person shares with other residents any accommodation (other than storage accommodation) on the premises; and

(c) the premises qualify as "small premises" (*i.e.* for six persons or two households).

Similarly it is unreasonable to withhold consent based upon sex: Sexual Discrimination Act 1975.

7. Section 22 of the Landlord and Tenant (Covenants) Act 1995 applies to qualified covenants against assignment of leases of commercial (not residential or agricultural) premises. The provision is designed to assist big commercial landlords and provides that a landlord may reasonably withhold consent to any assignment (not sub-letting or parting with possession) where the circumstances in which he may do so have been set out in an agreement and the circumstances anticipated in the agreement exist. Consequently, the landlord can stipulate in advance the circumstances in which he will grant consent to the assignment of a tenancy. The landlord may, for example, impose conditions about future guarantees or criteria for assessing the creditworthiness of any proposed assignee. Any veto will automatically be reasonable if within the terms of the agreement.

Methods of determination of leases

1. Expiry of the agreed period. In a lease for a fixed period, the tenancy will automatically determine when that period expires. This rule does not only apply to tenancies protected under various statutory schemes of protection.

2. Notice. This must be given in cases of periodic tenancies. A lease for a fixed period can only be determined by notice if the lease so provides. Break clauses may operate by notice, *e.g.* a 21-year lease determinable at the end of 7 or 14 years. Notice to quit served by one of several joint tenants can be valid: *Hammersmith & Fulham L.B.C. v. Monk* (1992). A notice to quit given by a tenant will automatically terminate any sub-tenancies which may have been granted by the tenant: *Pennell v. Payne* (1995).

3. Merger. This may arise where a tenant retains the lease and acquires the landlord's reversion, or where a third party acquires both. Both estates must be vested in one person, *i.e.* the interests merge, provided the parties intended this to occur: L.P.A., s.185.

4. Surrender. Where a tenant yields up his estate to the landlord this effects a merger in the reversion and the tenancy ends. A deed is required for an express surrender of a lease for greater than three years, though equity might need less formality. Surrender may also occur by operation of law, *e.g.* landlord accepting the return of the tenants' keys: *Chamberlaine v. Scally* (1992). Where a landlord releases a tenant from all obligations under a lease without any qualification or reservation, he also releases all the prior covenantors: *Deanplan v. Mahmoud* (1992).

5. Satisfied terms. A long term of years without rent may be created, *e.g.* to raise portions under a settlement. When the purpose of the term is satisfied the term ceases automatically under L.P.A. 1925, s.5.

6. Enlargement. Under L.P.A. 1925, s.153 a lease may be enlarged into a fee simple where the lease was originally for 300 years or more and there is still at least 200 years unexpired. There must be no trust or right of redemption in favour of the reversioner and the lease must not be liable to determination by re-entry for breach of condition. There must be no rent of any money value payable.

7. Disclaimer. This is a predominantly statutory right to repudiate where, *.e.g.* the property is rendered unfit by war damage, or under the Insolvency Act 1986, s.315: *London City Corp. v. Brown* (1990).

8. Forfeiture. The right to forfeit normally arises under a provision in the lease. A breach of covenant does not automatically give a right to forfeiture: the lease must contain a forfeiture clause, *i.e.* a clause giving the right to re-enter on breach of covenant: *Clarke v. Widmall* (1977). It is normal for leases to contain such a clause. The benefit of the landlord's right of re-entry will pass automatically to the assignees of the reversion under section 4 of the Landlord and Tenant (Covenants) Act 1995. Breach of a condition in the lease gives an automatic right to forfeiture.

   (a) Where a covenant (backed by a forfeiture clause) or a condition has been broken, this renders the lease voidable at the landlord's option.

   (b) A landlord may waive a breach of covenant, if, knowing the lease is liable to forfeiture, he does some act recognising its continued existence, *e.g.* sues for or accepts rent: *Central Estates v. Woolgar* (No. 2) (1972); *Re a Debtor* (1995). Waiver on one occasion does .not operate as a general waiver for the future: L.P.A.., s.148. Mere suspicion is not knowledge; *Chrisdell v. Johnson* (1987); compare *Van Haarlam v. Kasner* (1992).

Forfeiture procedures

The formalities required in a forfeiture action vary according to whether the covenant broken is for non-payment of rent which has a special procedure, as compared with any other covenant.

Non-payment of rent. 1. If not absolved by the lease the landlord must make a formal demand, *i.e.* he must personally or by authorised agent demand the exact sum on the precise day it falls due, at an hour before sunset which will enable him to count the money, such demand to be made on the demised premises until sunset. Normally the lease exempts the landlord from this procedure and under the Common Law Procedure Act 1852, s.210 the demand can be dispensed with if the rent is six months in arrears and any goods available for distress are not sufficient to satisfy all the arrears. For county court procedure: County Court Act 1984, s.138(9a) as amended by the Administration of Justice Act 1985, s.55(4).

2. A tenant may apply for relief within six months of the landlord's re-entry, such relief being granted on equitable grounds. Under-lessors have a similar right to relief under L.P.A. 1925, s.146(4).

Breach of other covenants and conditions. 1. This is governed by L.P.A., s.146, which provides that the landlord must serve on the tenant a notice which:

(a) specifies the breach complained of;

(b) requires it to be remedied if capable of being remedied.

After service of the notice the landlord must allow a reasonable period of time (usually three months) for compliance before effecting a re-entry. Any re-entry must be peaceable: Criminal Law Act 1977, s.6, as amended by the Criminal Justice and Public Order Act 1994, s.72, and it is usually advisable to obtain a court order by way of possession.

2. Certain covenants are incapable of remedy. In such cases the landlord need only specify the breach in serving the section 146 notice. The following are examples of irredeemable breaches:

(a) *Rugby School Governors v. Tannahill* (1935); breach of a covenant against illegal or immoral usage of property was held incapable of remedy after the premises were used for prostitution purposes; a stigma attached which could not be removed: *cf. Glass v. Kencakes* (1966).

(b) *Scala House and District Property Co. v. Forbes* (1974); once a covenant against assigning, sub-letting or parting with possession had been broken it was incapable of remedy. The general law on irredeemable breaches is reviewed in *Expert Clothing Service and Sales Ltd v. Hillgate House Ltd* (1986) and *Savva v. Houssein* (1996). In *Van Haarlam v. Kasner* (1992) it was held that using the premises for spying purposes was capable of remedy.

3. Where a covenant to repair has been broken, extra formalities need to be complied with:

(a) Landlord and Tenant Act 1927, s.18(2)—the notice must be made known to the tenant;

(b) Leasehold Properties Repair Act 1938—notification of tenant's rights to serve a counter-notice: See *Land Securities plc v. Receiver for the Metropolitan Police District* (1983).

A landlord cannot effect repairs himself and then serve a section 146 notice: *Sedac v. Tanner* (1982), though an action for debt against the tenant may succeed: *Hamilton v. Martell* (1984).

4. The tenant has a right to apply to the court for relief whilst

the landlord is proceeding to enforce his forfeiture, *i.e.* at any time before the landlord has actually re-entered the tenant may make his own application or apply in the landlord's action: s.146(2). A tenant may apply for relief after a landlord has forfeited by re-entry without first obtaining a court order for that purpose but the court in deciding whether to grant relief will take into account all the circumstances: *Billsom v. Residential Apartments Ltd* (1992).

5. Notice under section 146 is not required and forfeiture is automatic:

(a) on forfeiture for denial of title;

(b) breach of covenant in a mining lease to allow inspection of the mine's books, accounts, etc.;

(c) breach of a condition against bankruptcy of the tenant where the lease is of: agricultural or pastoral land; mines or minerals; public house; furnished house; or property where the personal qualifications of the tenant are important.

6. Sub-tenants may apply for relief against forfeiture of the interest of the head lease on any ground including non-payment of rent: L.P.A. 1925, s.146(4): *Escalus v. Dennis* (1995). Even if the tenant himself cannot apply for relief this does not preclude an application from the sub-tenant. If relief is granted the landlord may be required to grant a term direct to the sub-tenant for a period not exceeding that which the tenant originally held. The court may also have a general equitable jurisdiction: *Abbey National Building Society v. Maybeech Ltd* (1985). Contrast *Smith v. Metropolitan City Properties Ltd* (1986).

ENFORCEABILITY OF COVENANTS IN LEASES

This is an area of the law which has undergone significant changes by virtue of the Landlord and Tenant (Covenants) Act 1995. The Act became operative on January 1, 1996 and applies in the main to leases that are created after that date. The Act does not apply to pre–1996 leases or to those leases granted after that date but in pursuance of an agreement or court order made before it.

Rules for leases created before 1996

1. Original parties to the lease. Between the original parties to the lease there is *privity of contract* and all covenants are enforceable throughout the term in spite of any assignments. The landlord can enforce against the tenant even if some other person is liable by way of privity of estate. This liability extends only for the duration of the contractual term. An original tenant will not be liable on covenants where an assignee extends his term under the Landlord and Tenant Act 1954, s.24(1): *City of London Corporation v. Fell* (1993).

Certain provisions of the 1996 Act apply even where the lease was created before 1996 (ss. 17–20).

(a) Where an original tenant has become liable for the acts of an assignee, and has made full payment in respect of that liability, he may call for an overriding lease which will put him in the position of landlord to the defaulting assignee: s.19. The consequence of this is that the original tenant can deal with the property with a view to recovering some of the money paid out. It gives the original tenant control over the defaulting tenant, when he can sue for outstanding rent or damages for breach of contract and potentially forfeiture of the lease.

(b) The Act applies to pre–1996 leases where a covenant has been varied. Under s.18 a former tenant will not be liable to pay any amount resulting from a variation of a covenant occurring after the assignment. Whether this section was necessary can be doubted in the light of *Friends Provident Life Office v. British Railways Board* (1996) which clarified the common law position.

(c) Under s.17 the liability of a former tenant is limited in respect of any covenant under which a fixed charge is payable. The tenant is not responsible under the fixed charge covenant unless the landlord has served a notice, in the prescribed form, informing him that any charge is due within six months of the date it becomes due. A fixed charge includes rent, service charges and liquidated sums for breach of covenant.

The same general principles of enforceability apply to the landlord, who will normally remain liable on covenants following an assignment of the reversion.

2. Assignees of the lease. On a transfer of the lease by way of assignment, the issue arises as to whether the covenants run with the land and are enforceable by and against the assignee. A similar problem arises on an assignment of the reversion. Enforceability here depends upon the existence of *privity of estate*, whether the covenants "touch and concern" the land and whether the lease is in due form: *Boyer v. Warbey* (1953): *City of London Corporation v. Fell* (1994).

(a) Privity of estate exists wherever there is a landlord and tenant relationship under the lease in question.

(b) Covenants "touching and concerning" the land or "having reference to the subject matter of the grant": L.P.A. 1925, ss.141 and 142, are those which relate to the land itself and are not merely personal in nature. The criterion seems to be whether the covenant affects the landlord in his normal capacity as landlord or the tenant in his normal capacity as tenant (Cheshire). Covenants by the tenant to pay rent or repair would "touch and concern" the land, but a covenant to pay rates on other land would not. A covenant by the landlord to renew the lease would "touch and concern", but not a covenant to sell the reversion at a stated price at the tenants' option. A covenant does not "touch and concern" merely because its breach will cause forfeiture.

A covenant of surety or guarantee "touches and concerns" the land: *Kumar v. Dunning* (1987); *P & A Swift Investments v. Combined English Stores* (1988). Contrast *Hua Chiao Commercial Bank v. Chiaphua Industries* (1987) where it was held that a landlord's obligation to return a substantial security deposit, repayable at the end of a term, was merely personal and did not touch and concern the land. The meaning of s.141 L.P.A. 1925 was recently discussed in *Caerns v. Geddes* (1995).

Examples

  (i) L grants a lease by deed to T for 10 years. T then assigns the lease to X. The *benefit* of all covenants that "touch and concern" the land will pass to X under the rule in *Spencer's case* (1583), so that X can sue L direct on those covenants.

 (ii) On the same facts L can sue X provided the covenants "touch and concern" the land: L.P.A. 1925, s.79.

(iii) L grants a lease by deed to T for 10 years. L then assigns his reversion to R. There is privity of estate between R and T and under L.P.A. 1925, ss.141 and 142, the benefit and burden of all covenants "having reference to the subject matter of the grant" will pass. Consequently T can sue R and R can sue T on any covenant which relates to the land.

(c) Under L.P.A. 1925, s.141, an assignee of the reversion acquires the right to sue a tenant for breaches of covenant committed before the assignment (whether the covenant is of a continuous nature or not). This right exists even though there was no privity between the parties at the time of the breach: *London and County (A. & D.) Ltd v. Wilfred Sportsman Ltd* (1971); *Arlesford Trading Co. Ltd v. Servansingh* (1971). It was held in *City & Metropolitan Properties v. Greycroft* (1987) that a former tenant can sue the landlord for a loss that occurred while he was a tenant, even though the lease has since been assigned.

3. No privity of contract or estate. Generally covenants are unenforceable except:
   (a) the benefit but not the burden may be assigned with the land;
   (b) the burden of restrictive covenants may be transferred in equity.

4. The right to sue—indemnities. Privity of contract continues to exist between the original parties despite any assignments; thus the original tenant remains liable even if the landlord recognises the assignee as tenant. An assignee is only liable, or entitled, by virtue of privity of estate, and is only affected by matters during the time he has the estate (in the absence of a covenant for the future). The landlord has an option of suing the original tenant (privity of contract) or the tenant for the time being (privity of estate). The tenant for the time being is the principal debtor and the original tenant the surety. If the landlord chooses to sue the original tenant that tenant may recover from an assignee.
   (a) by way of any express indemnity inserted in the assignment;
   (b) under the implied indemnity provided in L.P.A. 1925, s.77(1)(c), where there has been an assignment for valuable consideration.
Where there has been a breach in the chain of indemnities, the original tenant may be able to recover directly from the tenant who causes the breach under the rule in *Moule v. Garrett* (1872). Here the law implies an obligation between joint debtors to repay money paid by one of them for the exclusive benefit of the other where both are liable to a common creditor (a rule of quasi-contract adapted to cover this situation): *Becton Dickinson U.K. Ltd v. Zwebner* (1988). The difficulties that can arise where members of a chain of assignments become insolvent are highlighted in the decision in *Re Mirror Group (Holdings) Ltd* (1993).

5. Sub-tenants: there is no direct relationship of privity of contract or estate between a landlord and a sub-tenant so that as a general rule neither can sue the other directly on covenants in the lease (sub-lease). Exceptions to this rule arise:

(a) where a restrictive covenant is contained in the head lease, this can be sued upon directly under the rule in *Tulk v. Moxhay* (1848);

(b) where the right of re-entry in the head lease is exercised, this may forfeit the sub-lease, though a claim for relief is possible.

The position in respect of tenancies created after 1996 is amended by s.3(5) of the Landlord and Tenant (Covenants) Act 1995 and is dealt with in the following section.

Rule for leases created after 1996

The rules on enforceability of covenants were uncertain and inconsistent and prompted criticism from many quarters. In particular, the Law Commission Report on "Landlord and Tenant Law: Privity of Contract and Estate" (No. 174) and see the views of Beldam L.J. in *Norwich Union Life Insurance v. Low Profile Fashions* (1992).

The major point of criticism was the continuing liability of the original tenant throughout the lease and the potential liability on such tenants for breaches of covenant committed after an assignment of the lease had taken place. The injustices this caused were remedied by the Landlord and Tenant (Covenants) Act 1995. This is a major new statute and makes fundamental changes to the law.

1. The Act will apply to all new tenancies created after January 1, 1996 save for those sections (ss. 17–20) that apply to all tenancies.

2. The Act applies to both legal and equitable leases: s.28(1).

3. The fundamental principle contained in the Act is that a tenant (whether original or an assignee) who assigns the lease is released from the burden of leasehold covenants and ceases to be entitled to the landlord covenants after the assignment: s.5.

4. The Act applies to both landlord covenants and tenant covenants whether or not they have reference to the subject matter of the tenancy and whether the covenant is express, implied or imposed by law: ss.2 and 3.

5. Although a tenant may cease to be liable on covenants after an assignment the landlord may require a tenant who wishes to assign to give a guarantee for his immediate assignee by entering into an "authorised guarantee agreement" which guarantees the performance of the covenants by the assignee: s.16.

6. If only part of the property is assigned, then the tenant will be released from any covenants that relate to that part. Where a

covenant is not attributable to any part of the property that is being assigned then the landlord and tenant can enter into a contract as to the apportionment of liability: s.9.

7. Section 6 of the Act provides that a landlord (whether original or an assignee) is not automatically released from his covenants on the assignment of the reversion. Under s.8 the landlord may serve a notice on the tenant informing him of the assignment and requesting release from the covenants. The release will be effective if the tenant consents or does not reply within the specified period or on the landlord's application to the court.

8. There are a number of situations where a landlord or tenant may not be released from their liability under agreed covenants. These are known as "excluded assignments" and include:

(a) assignments on breach of a covenant in the tenancy, *e.g.* an assignment in breach of a covenant against assignment; and

(b) assignments by operation of law, *e.g.* an assignment on the death of a joint tenant of the legal estate.

The effect of an excluded assignment is to defer the release of the tenant from liability to the next assignment which is not an excluded assignment: s.11. Any term in a lease expressed to be made personal to a named person will not be released to the assignee on an assignment.

9. The terms of the Act appear to lean heavily in favour of the tenant and expose a landlord to the potential unscrupulous assignee. To an extent this is mitigated by the requirement that the tenant, in certain circumstances, is required to guarantee the performance of the covenants by the assignee. The introduction of the "authorised guarantee agreement" will give some protection to the landlord. Section 16(3) lays down the conditions as to when a tenant is required to enter into an authorised guarantee assignment:

(a) it depends on the nature of the covenant against assignment. Where there is an absolute or qualified covenant against assignment, then such a guarantee may be imposed. Where the tenant is free to assign without the landlord's consent then the guarantee cannot be imposed;

(b) where such consent to assignment is given, it is made subject to a condition that the tenant is to enter into an agreement guaranteeing the performance by the assignee;

(c) the agreement is entered into in pursuance of that condition.

The authorised guarantee agreement may impose on the tenant:

(a) liability as sole or principal debtor of the assignee's obligations;

(b) liability as a guarantor of the assignee providing the liabilities are not greater than those imposed on the assignee;

(c) the obligation, where the tenancy is disclaimed, to take on any new lease for the duration of the term.

10. The position of sub-tenants in leases effective after 1996 is covered by s.3(5) of the Act in relation to restrictive covenants.

> "Any landlord or tenant covenant of a tenancy which is restrictive of the user of land shall, as well as being capable of enforcement against an assignee, be capable of being enforced against any other person who is the owner or occupier of any demised premises to which the covenant relates, even though there is no express provision in the tenancy to that effect."

Under this provision direct enforcement against the sub-tenant is permitted. The extent of this provision and its relationship to the rule in *Tulk v. Moxhay* (1848) will need to be worked out by the courts.

Statutory protected tenancies

The tenant under a lease is given certain protections by the law, mainly relating to levels of rent and restrictions on the landlord's ability to regain possession of the property. The nature of the protection varies according to the type of tenancy created. Students should refer principally to the Rent Act 1977 and the Housing Act 1988 for the provisions.

---

6. SETTLEMENTS AND TRUSTS FOR SALE

Introduction

Traditionally successive interests in land could be created in two main ways: by way of a strict settlement under the Settled Land Act 1925, or alternatively by way of a trust for sale under the Law of Property Act 1925. The machinery and administration of these two systems differ greatly and is outmoded and unduly complex. Consequently the Trusts of Land and Appointment of Trustees Act 1996 (the 1996 Act) has made far reaching and substantial changes to the law.

The Act came into force on January 1, 1997 and its provisions need careful consideration as they impact on many aspects of the law relating to land. The Act prevents the creation of any new strict settlements (with minor exceptions) though existing settlements will continue to operate under the old rules. The trust for sale has been, to all intents and purposes, abolished and existing trusts for sale will be converted to the new "trusts of land". All new attempts to create successive interests in land must take effect under the machinery of the trust of land: ss.4 and 5.

New powers are created in favour of the trustees of land who are to have the same powers as the person who owns the estate or interest in the land not subject to a trust, but subject to their obligations as trustees: s.6.

Given that existing settlements are to continue to operate under the old rules, it is necessary to be familiar with those rules in addition to understanding how the new provisions will operate. A summary of the law relating to strict settlements and trusts for sale will be undertaken followed by the new provisions under the 1996 Act.

Strict settlement

1. This is a mechanism which describes an arrangement which establishes a series of successive beneficial interests in favour of a number of persons. A simple example would be where Blackacre is left by a settlor to B for life, remainder to C in fee simple. A settlement usually comes into existence on the occasion of marriage or a death and was used in former times to keep land in the family. In the above example the person who creates a settlement is known as the settlor. B is the tenant for life, who holds the legal estate and is beneficially entitled for his lifetime. He has extensive powers of management and disposition given by the L.P.A. 1925. C is the remainderman who will become absolutely entitled to the property when B dies. Trustees of the settlement will often be appointed by the instrument of creation.

Trust for sale

1. A trust for sale was a trust which directed the trustees to sell the trust property, invest the proceeds and hold the resulting funds upon the trusts declared by the settlor. A simple example would be where S conveyed Blackacre to X and Y (Trustees) on trust to sell the land and to hold the proceeds for the benefit of B for life, then to C absolutely. Under such a trust for sale the trustees held the legal estate and the powers of management and control of the property were vested in them and not the tenant for life. The trust

for sale treated the property as money (conversion) and this enabled easy distribution of the property. The mechanism was also convenient for distributing both land and personalty together.

2. A trust for sale and a settlement were mutually exclusive and could not exist at the same time in respect of the same property: Settled Land Act 1925, s.1(7).

SETTLED LAND

Definition

1. Since the general policy of the Settled Land Act 1925 was to give wide powers to all "limited owners", the existence of almost any limited interest in land indicated a settlement. A settlement could be created by any document or series of documents where land was for the time being:
   (a) limited in trust for any persons by way of succession;
   (b) by way of an entail;
   (c) for an estate in fee simple or a term of years absolute subject to an executory limitation;
   (d) for a base or determinable fee;
   (e) in the case of an infant, for an estate in fee simple or a term of years absolute (a person under 18 cannot hold a legal estate in land and the trustees hold on his behalf);
   (f) limited in trust for any persons for an estate in fee simple or for a term of years absolute contingently on the happening of any event, *e.g.* "to the first daughter of Sam who shall marry";
   (g) charged by way of a family arrangement.

Creation of a settlement

After 1925 all settlements had to be made by two documents, namely a trust instrument and a vesting deed; S.L.A. 1925, s.4(1).

1. Trust instrument. This contains the trusts (*i.e.* the beneficial interests of the settlement); these being normally of no concern to the purchaser of a legal estate they are now kept off the legal title. This is a private document. Where a settlement is created by will, the will is treated as the trust instrument.

The instrument normally contains according to S.L.A. 1925, s.4(3):
   (a) a declaration of the trusts affecting the settled land;
   (b) appointment of the trustees;
   (c) the power, if any, to appoint new trustees;

(d) any additional powers for the tenant for life;

(e) a provision for bearing *ad valorem* stamp duty.

2. Vesting deed (assent). This is a public document which is of principal concern to a purchaser. Under S.L.A. 1925, s.5(1), it must contain:

(a) a description of the settled land either specifically or generally;

(b) a declaration that the settled land is vested in the person or persons to whom it is conveyed or in whom it is declared to be vested, upon the trusts affecting the settled land;

(c) a statement of the names of the trustees;

(d) any additional powers given by the trust instrument to the tenant for life;

(e) the names of persons entitled to appoint new trustees.

The vesting deed usually keeps the trusts entirely off the title to the legal estate and thus the legal estate can be dealt with by a purchaser without reference to the trusts; in fact the S.L.A. 1925, s.110(2) compels a purchaser to take the vesting instrument at its face value.

3. Where a settlement was created before 1926, when it was possible to create a settlement by way of a single document, that document is treated as the trust instrument and a vesting deed should be executed by the trustees in favour of the tenant for life as soon as practicable.

4. Improperly constituted settlements. Where a tenant for life or statutory owners are entitled to have the legal estate vested in them by way of a vesting instrument, then any purported disposition of the legal estate before the execution of the vesting instrument will be ineffective, except in favour of a purchaser of a legal estate who has no notice of the settlement: S.L.A. 1925, s.13 (known as the paralysing section). The object of the section is to make the tenant for life obtain a proper vesting instrument and where he does not do so and attempts to deal with the legal estate, such disposition operates as a contract to transfer the legal estate and as such is a registrable estate contract.

The paralysing effect of section 13 does not operate:

(a) where the settlement has come to an end before the execution of a vesting instrument; *Re Alexfounders W.T.* (1927);

(b) where there has been a disposition by a personal representative;

(c) where a person of full age is beneficially entitled to land subject to family charges. Here he may sell the land subject to the charges as though it were not settled land (no vesting deed required): L.P. (Amendment) Act 1926, s.1.

Trustees of the settlement

1. The trustees of a settlement are, in order of priority, laid down by S.L.A. 1925, s.30.
   (a) persons under a settlement with a power of sale;
   (b) persons declared by a settlement to be trustees "for the purpose of the Settled Land Act";
   (c) trustees of any other land in the same settlement which is subject to the same limitations;
   (d) persons with a future power of sale;
   (e) persons appointed by beneficiaries, provided they are of full capacity.
2. If a settlement arises on a death the personal representatives are trustees until others are appointed: S.L.A. 1925, s.30(3).
3. The court has a residuary discretion to appoint trustees where appropriate: S.L.A. 1925, s.34.
4. The functions of trustees are:
   (a) to act as the statutory owners where there is no tenant for life; or as "special statutory owners" on the death of a tenant for life;
   (b) to give consents to certain transactions of the tenant for life; and to receive notice of when the tenant for life is exercising certain other transactions or powers;
   (c) to receive and hold capital money;
   (d) to execute vesting documents and documents of discharge;
   (e) to conduct the powers of the tenant for life where he wishes to purchase the land; or where he has unreasonably refused to exercise his statutory powers and a court order directs the trustees to act.

THE TENANT FOR LIFE—DEFINITION

1. The tenant for life is the person under the settlement who has all the statutory powers of management and control as well as possessing the legal estate: S.L.A. 1925, s.177(1). He is the person of full age who is for the time being beneficially entitled to possession of the settled land for his life: S.L.A. 1925, s.19(1). Section 20 of the Act extends the definition to a variety of other persons having a limited beneficial interest in possession. This virtually includes

any person of full age with, for example, an entailed interest, or a fee simple subject to a gift over, or to family charges.

2. In certain cases, for example, where the person entitled is an infant, there may be no tenant for life within the statutory definition. The powers of the tenant for life are then exercised by the "statutory owners," who are usually the trustees of the settlement. If in any case there are two more persons of full age so entitled as joint tenants, they together constitute the tenant for life for the purposes of the Settled Land Act 1925: *Muir v. Lloyds Bank plc* (1992).

Powers of the tenant for life

1. The tenant for life can in general deal with his own limited interest as he pleases, but transactions will not bind his successors. As to the legal estate which is vested in him he can make no disposition except as permitted by the Act: S.L.A. 1925, s.18. The tenant for life is trustee not only of his powers but also of the legal estate vested in him.

2. Some of the powers enumerated below must not be exercised without notice being given to the trustees of the settlement: S.L.A. 1925, s.101(1). This applies to the tenant for life's powers to sell; exchange; lease; mortgage or charge; or grant an option. He must give one month's notice before the transaction or contract in such cases. The notice must be given to two or more trustees or a trust corporation. Section 101 may be of little value because the trustees need not interfere with improper transactions, they may waive notice and the notice required may need to be in general form only, except for mortgaging or charging the land. A purchaser dealing bona fide with the tenant for life need not inquire whether notice has been given: S.L.A. 1925, ss.110(4), 117(1)(XXI).

3. The power to sell or exchange: S.L.A., s.39(1): the best consideration reasonably obtainable is required. A purchaser who is acting in good faith with the tenant for life is deemed to have given the best consideration reasonably obtainable and is protected against S.L.A. 1925, s.18 which invalidates irregular transactions by a tenant for life or statutory owners. Where joint tenants constitute the tenant for life and one wants to sell and the other doesn't the court will not order sale in the absence of bad faith: *Re 90 Thornhill Road* (1970).

4. Power to grant leases: given by S.L.A., s.41 within the following limits:

(a) building and forestry—999 years;
(b) mining—100 years;

(c) any other—50 years.

5. Power to raise money on mortgage: Settled Land Act, s.71 specifies several purposes for which the settled land may be mortgaged;
   (a) discharge of an incumbrance on the land;
   (b) payment for any improvement authorised by S.L.A. 1925 or the settlement;
   (c) equality of exchange;
   (d) payment of costs of any of the above.

6. Power to grant options. They must be in writing at the best price or rent, provided they are not exercisable after 10 years.

Consent of trustees

The consent of the trustees is required before the tenant for life can exercise the following rights:

1. Sale of a principal mansion house: consent is required in two situations:
   (a) in a pre-1926 settlement which does not dispense with such leave; or
   (b) in a post-1925 settlement expressly requiring such leave: S.L.A. 1925, s.65.

2. The power to cut and sell timber: S.L.A. 1925, s.66.

3. The power to compromise claims: S.L.A. 1925, s.58(1).

Consent of the court

A court order is required before the tenant for life can exercise the following rights:

1. The right to sell heirlooms: all proceeds are capital: S.L.A. 1925, s.67.

2. The power to effect any transaction which in the opinion of the court would be for the benefit of the settled land or beneficiaries: *Re White Popham* (1936).

Section 64 S.L.A. permits a tenant for life to carry out any transaction under an order of the court: *Hambro v. Duke of Marlborough* (1994)—variation of the beneficial interest of an adult beneficiary.

Consent of the trustees or of the court

1. Such consents are required to effect certain improvements of the settled land and to defray the cost out of capital or for it to be raised by mortgage. If the improvements are not authorised they must be paid for out of income. The precise details of financing vary according to permanency of benefit according to the classification imposed by Schedule 3 to the S.L.A. 1925.

(a) Part I improvements, of lasting benefit such as drainage, irrigation and bridges can be financed out of capital and the tenant for life need not pay for them personally.

(b) Part II improvements are of a more doubtful lasting benefit, *e.g.* provision of houses for agents; repair of dry rot; boring for water. Here the trustees or the court have a discretion as to whether to request the setting up of a sinking fund requiring payment out of income.

(c) Part III improvements are of a transitory value, *e.g.* installation of electricity or the purchase of farm vehicles. The trustees must require repayment for such improvements.

Attempted limitation of the powers of the tenant for life

1. The Settled Land Act makes all powers (with minor exceptions) exercisable only by the tenant for life. The settlement may supplement the powers given by the Act but cannot curtail them. Section 106 makes void any provision which attempts to prevent or discourage the tenant for life from exercising his statutory powers. The section expressly includes attempts to discourage or prevent by some limitation of *other* real or personal property. Any requirement that the tenant for life:

(a) should forfeit his interest in the land if for example he should exercise his power of sale or exchange is invalid;

(b) requires the consent of any third person before exercising the statutory powers of sale or exchange is similarly invalid.

2. Any provision is void only so far as it in fact "tends to prevent or discourage the exercise of the statutory powers.' Thus, for example, a provision that the tenant for life shall forfeit his interest if he ceases to reside on the settled land for some purpose other than the exercise of his statutory powers is not void, but if he ceases to reside because he has sold or leased the property the forfeiture provision is inoperative: *Re Acklom* (1929); *Re Ames* (1893). A problematic situation arises where a settlor provides a fund to be used for the maintenance and upkeep of the settled land whilst the tenant for life is in occupation. The prospect of losing such a fund may dissuade the tenant for life from exercising his powers of leasing or selling and consequently may be void. The authorities are, however, conflicting and it seems that such a fund can be retained if the land is leased but not sold: *Re Aberconway's S.T.* (1953); *Re Simpson* (1913); *Re Patten* (1929).

Non-assignability of the powers of the tenant for life

A tenant for life cannot relinquish his powers: S.L.A. 1925, s.104, even if he has parted with his own beneficial interest, unless:

(a) the tenant for life has surrendered his interest to the person next entitled under the settlement, so as to extinguish his own interest. The powers here are exercisable as if he were dead: S.L.A., s.105;

(b) the tenant for life has ceased to have a substantial beneficial interest (whether by bankruptcy, assignment, incumbrance or otherwise), and has unreasonably refused to exercise the powers or consents to an order. The court may, on application of anyone interested, make an order authorising the trustees to exercise the statutory powers; *Re Thornhill Settlement* (1941);

(c) the tenant for life is a mental patient, the statutory powers being exercised by order of the Court of Protection.

Acquisition of the settled land by the tenant for life

If the tenant for life wishes to acquire any or all of the settled land for himself, by virtue of S.L.A. 1925, s.68 the trustees take over all the powers of the tenant for life to negotiate and complete any such transaction.

Protection of purchasers

Where a tenant for life completes a transaction by way of exercising his statutory powers such as selling or leasing the settled land, the interests of beneficiaries under the settlement are overreached. In dealing with any purchaser the tenant for life must ensure that the best price reasonably obtainable has been obtained, that the purchase money has been paid to at least two trustees and the provisions regarding vesting instruments and notice have been complied with. Such complicated formalities might well deter a purchaser from buying settled land if the Settled Land Act did not exclude him from establishing that they had all been observed. The following statutory provisions protect the position of the purchaser:

(a) S.L.A. 1925, s.110: a purchaser acting in good faith shall be deemed to have given the best price obtainable and to have complied with all the provisions of the Act. This provision applies whether or not the purchaser realises that he is dealing with a tenant for life; *Re Morgan's Lease* (1972), though this view appears to conflict with the decision in *Weston v. Henshaw* (1950). The apparent conflict was not settled by the recent decision in *Bevan v. Johnson* (1990). The opportunity for the courts to consider sections 18, 110 and 112 of the S.L.A. arose but was not taken by the Court of Appeal in this case.

　(b) S.L.A. 1925, s.110(2): a purchaser of a legal estate is not
　　　entitled to call for the trust instrument but may assume that
　　　certain particulars stated in the vesting deed are true.
　(c) S.L.A. 1925, s.101: a person dealing in good faith with the
　　　tenant for life is not concerned whether notice of an intended
　　　transaction has been given to the trustees.
　(d) S.L.A. 1925, s.95: the purchaser is not concerned as to how
　　　the proceeds of sale paid to the trustees are distributed.
　(e) S.L.A. 1925, s.18: any disposition by the tenant for life or
　　　statutory owners which is not authorised by the Act is void
　　　except for the purpose of binding the tenant for life's own
　　　beneficial interest while it continues. *N.B.* interrelationship
　　　with "paralysing" effect of section 13.

S.L.A. 1925, s.5(3): a vesting deed will not be invalid because of
any error in any of the statements or particulars required to be
within it.

Settlements and licences

There has been a degree of overlap and uncertainty by the courts
as to whether certain limitations give rise to settlements or create
only a species of licence. For example, in *Bannister v. Bannister*
(1948), B, the owner of two cottages, conveyed them to her brother-
in-law at a reduced price, on the understanding that she would
remain in one of them rent free. It was held that a life interest in
the property had been created and B was a tenant for life under the
Settled Land Act 1925. Similarly in *Binions v. Evans* (1972), trustees
agreed to allow a widow to occupy a cottage "for the remainder of
her life as a tenant at will rent free." This was held to create a
settlement and the widow was the tenant for life.

In *Ungurian v. Lesnoff* (1989), L gave up her home and job in
Poland to come to England to live with U. U purchased a house
where the parties lived together with the children from their previous relationships. L did this on the understanding that she would
live there indefinitely. The house was in U's name alone although
L renovated it extensively. The relationship broke down. It was
held that U held the house on a constructive trust for L, who was
a tenant for life under the Settled Land Act 1925.

These decisions have been questioned in that:

　(a) the powers given to a tenant for life under the Settled Land
　　　Act 1925, *e.g.* sale, leasing, could not have been within the
　　　expectation of the parties;
　(b) the factual situations are difficult to fit within the definition
　　　of a settlement;

(c) there is lack of documentary evidence, *i.e.* no writing. This mitigates against the existence of a settlement;

(d) the courts seem to be confusing a right to reside (licence) and a right to use and occupy (estate in land).

TRUST FOR SALE

With the coming into force of the Trusts of Land and Appointment of Trustees Act 1996 the trust for sale mechanism has been replaced by the trust of land even in respect of existing trusts for sale. To understand the nature of the changes it is necessary to understand how the mechanisms of the trust for sale operated.

Definition

A trust for sale was defined in section 205(1)(XXIX) of the Law of Property Act 1925 as "an immediate binding trust for sale": see also S.L.A. 1925, s.117(1)(XXX). In terms of this definition:

1. Trust for sale. This emphasised the imperative aspect of the trust and clearly distinguished it from a power of sale which was discretionary. Perhaps misleadingly a trust "to retain or sell the land" was treated as a trust for sale with a power of postponement: L.P.A. 1925, s.25(4).

2. Immediate. This prevented a trust for sale at some future date being within the definition, for example, "when X attains the age of 25." Here a strict settlement was created. A trust for sale could be immediate even if the sale could not be made without the consent of some particular person: *Re Herklots W.T.* (1964). Implied in every trust for sale, other than where there was a contrary intention, was the power to postpone sale: L.P.A., s.25. The meaning of "immediate" in relation to gifts by will was considered in *Muir v. Lloyds Bank* (1992).

3. Binding. This merely emphasised that it was an obligation to sell and not a discretionary power; however, some dispute existed as to its exact meaning. Several interpretations were put forward:

(a) it emphasised the trustee's power to convey the land so that all equitable interests prior to the trust were overreached; *Re Leigh's S.E.* (1926);

(b) it excluded a mere revocable trust; *Re Parker's S.E.* (1928);

(c) it emphasised the imperative trust of the entire legal estate.

Creation

A trust for sale could arise either expressly or by operation of a statute.

1. Expressly. This arose in a will or by an *inter vivos* transaction. Two documents were often used, though not always. The trust instrument determined the beneficial interests and the conveyance transferred the legal estate to the trustees. Under a will, the will itself was the trust instrument and a vesting document by the personal representatives vested the legal estate in the trustees.

2. Statutory. Because the trust for sale was a mechanism for conveniently distributing property, statutes imposed a trust for sale:

(a) under the Administration of Estates Act 1925, s.33(1) which provided that all property whether real or personal which did not consist of money was held on a trust for sale on a death intestate;

(b) where co-ownership existed in the form of a joint tenancy or a tenancy in common: L.P.A. 1925, ss.34, 36;

(c) if trustees lent money on mortgage and the property became vested in them, *e.g.* on foreclosure.

Powers of the trustees for sale

1. Unless a contrary intention existed the trustees under a trust for sale created after 1925 had the power to postpone sale: L.P.A., s.25, though the court at their discretion could overrule this and order sale at the instance of any interested party: L.P.A. 1925, s.30. Where the power to postpone had been excluded one year was regarded as a reasonable period in which to sell. Where there was a dispute among the trustees as to whether the land shall be sold or not, it was to be sold even if this was contrary to the majority view: *Re Mayo* (1943). Consequently, all trustees had to agree to a postponement. Where there was a statutory trust for sale the trustees were under an obligation to consult the beneficiaries and give effect to the majority wishes, calculated in accordance with the majority holding: L.P.A. 1925, s.26(3). This provision did not seem to apply to an express trust for sale.

2. The court would not order a sale if this defeated the object for which the trust for sale was established, for example, a family or matrimonial home: *Jones v. Challenger* (1961), or where it defeated the common intention of the parties: *Re Buchanan–Wollaston's Conv.* (1939).

3. The trustees had all the powers of the tenant for life under the Settled Land Act as well as the Settled Land Act trustees: L.P.A. 1925, s.28(1).

4. Trustees had to obtain all consents in accordance with the terms of the trust on penalty of breach of trust, though any purchaser needed only to check that two consents had been obtained, even though the trust required more: L.P.A. 1925, s.26(1).

5. The trustees could delegate in writing certain management powers such as leasing or accepting surrenders to any person beneficially entitled in possession: L.P.A. 1925, s.29(1).

The doctrine of conversion

1. The immediate effect of a trust for sale was that the beneficiary's interest in land was converted into money or personalty. This was based on the equitable maxim that "equity looks on that as done which ought to be done" and as the duty to sell was imperative the conversion occurred as from the moment the trust for sale arose. In *Re Kempthorne* (1930), a testator on his death left all his freehold and copyhold to X and all his personal property to Y. The testator was entitled to an undivided share in land on his death. It was held that this passed as personal property to Y because of the doctrine of conversion.

2. In theory the principle of overreaching did not apply to a trust for sale because the beneficiary's interest was deemed to be in the purchase money from the outset, though the purchase money still had to be paid to at least two trustees or a trust corporation for a purchaser to take free of the rights of beneficiaries: L.P.A. 1925, s.27(2).

Trusts for sale and registered land

1. The legal estate had to be registered in the names of the trustees for sale where the trust for sale was of registered land. The normal rule prevailed that there can be no more than four who were of full age and capacity: Land Registration Act 1925, s.94(1).

2. On registration, the registrar entered a restriction protecting the beneficiary's minor interest by requiring that any purchase moneys must be paid to at least two trustees or a trust corporation, unless the registrar or the court otherwise directed. Compliance with the restriction overrode the interests of the beneficiaries by analogy with the overreaching provisions dealing with settled land in unregistered conveyancing.

3. A beneficiary in actual occupation or in receipt of rent and

profits had an overriding interest under L.R.A. 1925, s.70(1) thereby giving independent protection under the trust for sale: *Williams & Glyn's Bank Ltd v. Boland* (1981).

TRUSTS OF LAND UNDER THE TRUSTS OF LAND AND APPOINTMENT OF TRUSTEES ACT 1996

Trusts of land

The general scheme of the Act is to replace the dual systems governing strict settlements and trusts for sale with a single flexible "trust of land". This has a considerable impact on many areas of land holding, but in particular land held in co-ownership.

1. The Act is based on the recommendations of the Law Commission on "Trusts of Land" (No. 181) and "Overreaching: Beneficiaries in Occupation" (No. 188) and came into force on January 1, 1997.

2. The Act defines a "trust of land" as "any trust of property which consists of or includes land" and trustees of land mean trustees of a trust of land. The Act applies to all forms of trust (express, implied, resulting and constructive) including a trust for sale and a bare trust.

3. The creation of new strict settlements is prohibited but existing settlements continue. Resettlements and settlements created under powers of appointment given by existing settlements are outside the prohibition and charitable, ecclesiastical and public trusts of land are all trusts of land, whenever they were created: s.2.

4. The creation of entailed interests is no longer possible though existing ones continue. Any attempt to create an entailed interest after 1997 will create a fee simple, provided the grantor has this interest.

5. The doctrine of conversion is abolished and beneficiaries under the trust of land hold an interest in land and not in money: s.3. One consequence of this is that undivided shares in land are now within the definition of land in the L.P.A. s.205(1)(*ix*).

6. Express and statutorily implied trusts now share mainly the same characteristics: s.4. One of the main consequences of this change is that the power to postpone sale by the trustees is inviolable, and cannot be negatived. There is now no duty to sell, where previously there was under a trust for sale.

Powers of trustees of land

The powers of trustees under the L.P.A., s.28 governing trusts for sale, and under the Settled Land Act governing strict settlements were complicated, fragmented and often limited. Under the 1996 Act the legal title will be vested in the trustees and they will have all the powers of an absolute owner for the purpose of exercising their functions as trustees.

1. In exercising their powers the trustees shall have regard to the rights of the beneficiaries. The trustees are under a duty to consult beneficiaries (beneficially entitled to an interest in possession) and give effect to their wishes, in so far as is consistent with the purposes of the trust of land: ss.6:11.

2. There is a new statutory power to purchase land and a revised one to partition: ss.6 and 7.

3. The powers of the trustees may be made subject to the consent of the equitable owners, *i.e.* a tenant for life or persons entitled in remainder but only if this is provided in the trust instrument or by order of the court.

4. The overreaching machinery will apply to trusts of land in the same way as previously in respect of co-ownership trusts of land.

5. Trustees of land may delegate to beneficiaries much the same powers as a tenant for life has under a strict settlement: s.9.

6. Under the old law it was common to find that trustees for sale could not actually sell land subject to a trust for sale without the consent of certain persons. Under the 1996 Act whatever the instrument creating the trust of land provides, no more than two consents are needed to be exercised by the trustees of any function relating to the land in order for a purchaser to be protected. Although a minor's consent is not necessary to protect a purchaser, the consent of a parent who has parental responsibility is required. The consent of a receiver of a mentally incapable person is required: s.10.

7. New rules on consultation with beneficiaries are provided in s.11. Trustees of land are required, so far as practicable, to consult the beneficiaries of full age and beneficially entitled to an interest in possession in the land when exercising any function relating to land subject to the trust. The trustees should, so far as is consistent with the general interest of the trust, give effect to the wishes of those beneficiaries or in case of dispute of the majority (according to the value of their combined interest): s.11. This effectively replaces s.26(3) L.P.A. 1925, though there are some differences.

Where a new trust of land is created, the creators of the trust can "opt out" of the consultation obligation, and similarly existing trusts can be "opted in".

Rights of occupation

A beneficiary who is beneficially entitled to an interest in possession in land is entitled by reason of his interest to occupy the land at any time provided the land is held by the trustees so as to be available and occupation is not inconsistent with the trust of land: s.12.

Powers of the court

Under s.14 of the 1996 Act the powers of the court have been extended so that the court may make orders not only relating to sale, or no sale, but including overriding consent requirements or imposing such requirements and covering any dispute about the exercise of any of the trustee's functions or about the nature or extent of beneficiaries' interests.

Section 15 of the Act gives a guideline as to the criteria to be used by the court in granting orders. This includes looking to the intentions of the creators of the trust; the purposes for which the property subject to the trust is held; the welfare of any minor who occupies or might reasonably be expected to occupy any land subject to the trust as a home and the interests of any secured creditor of any beneficiary. The decisions governing s.30 L.P.A. 1925 will still be relevant in indicating how the courts should exercise their discretion.

The s.14 procedure applies to trusts of proceeds of sale and land just as it applies to trusts of land.

Protection for purchasers

The overreaching provisions in s.27 L.P.A. 1925 still apply so that if a purchaser pays capital money to at least two trustees or a trust corporation his interest prevails over third party equitable interests under the trust for sale: s.16 of the 1996 Act. This applies only to unregistered land as the registered land system mechanisms provide their own protection.

Where a trust is being terminated and trustees are to convey unregistered land to a beneficiary, the trustees are required to execute a deed of discharge.

A purchaser will not need to check that trustees have obtained any consents required, made consultation of beneficiaries or are acting in the best interests of any beneficiaries.

It should be noted that the 1996 Act also makes new provisions for the appointment and retirement of trustees: Part II of the Act.

7. CO-OWNERSHIP

Co-ownership (concurrent interests) deals with cases where two or more persons are entitled to simultaneous enjoyment of land. A grant of Blackacre "to X and Y in fee simple" or "to X and Y in equal shares" creates co-ownership whereas where land is granted consecutively as "to X for life; then to Y in fee simple" this creates a settlement and no co-ownership exists. The law relating to co-ownership can be found in the common law rules, the structures of the 1925 property legislation and the new provisions of the Trusts of Land and Appointment of Trustees Act 1996.

TYPES OF CO-OWNERSHIP

There were four types of co-ownership in land prior to 1926:
   (a) joint tenancy;
   (b) tenancy in common;
   (c) tenancy by entireties;
   (d) coparcenary.
   Of these four types of co-ownership only the first two are of practical significance after 1925, in that tenancies by entireties were effectively abolished by the L.P.A. 1925, s.37 and Schedule, Pt. VI, and converted for all intents and purposes into joint tenancies. Coparcenary can only arise today in the rare circumstances of an unbarred entailed interest or in the case of a pre-1926 intestate lunatic.

Joint tenancy

   Although as between themselves joint tenants have separate rights, a against anyone else they are in the position of a single owner. The outstanding feature of the joint tenancy is the right of survivorship.

   1. Survivorship. On the death of one joint tenant, his interest in land passes to the others by right of survivorship (*jus accrescendi*) until eventually only one owner survives. This right is not ousted by a joint tenant's will or intestacy. Consequently a joint tenant may hold all or nothing.

   2. Unities. A joint tenancy cannot exist unless the unities exist.
   (a) Unity of possession. Prior to the 1996 Act any owner was as much entitled to possession of the whole and every part of

the property as any other. If one joint tenant insisted on the exclusive possession of any part, then the remedy was to apply for partition. One co-owner could not bring an action for trespass against any other co-owner. However, the practical effects of unity of possession have been modified by ss.12 and 13 of the 1996 Act in that there is now a statutory right to occupy in favour of a beneficiary and the trustees may exclude or restrict the entitlement of any beneficiary to occupy the land.

(b) Unity of interest: the interest of each joint tenant must be identical in extent, nature and duration. No joint tenancy is possible between a fee simple owner and a tenant for years. Similarly no joint tenant can sell or lease because he does not have the whole legal estate. Unity of interest need only apply to the estate held jointly; any further interest held by any joint tenant is irrelevant. Paradoxically a notice to quit given by one of several joint tenants may be valid: *Hammersmith and Fulham L.B.C. v. Monk* (1992).

(c) Unity of title: all joint tenants must claim title under the same act or document, for example, by the same conveyance or by the same act of adverse possession.

(d) Unity of time: the joint tenants' interests must all vest at the same time. This often follows from unity of title though not, for example, in the unusual case of a gift "to A for life; remainder to the heirs of B and C," since the heirs of B and C would be established at different times.

Consequences of a joint tenancy

A beneficial joint tenancy has the following features:

1. Each co-owner has a "potential" share in the property. If there are four co-owners, each has a potential one-quarter share of the proceeds of sale. They are entitled to any rents and profits pending sale in the same proportions.

2. The joint tenancy will continue until only one survivor is entitled to the land by way of survivorship.

3. Any joint-tenant can convert his joint tenancy into a tenancy in common by way of severance. (This is dealt with later.)

Tenancy in common

This form of co-ownership differs from a joint tenancy in the following ways:

1. Tenants in common hold in individual shares, *i.e.* they have distinct shares which have not yet been divided.

2. There is no right of survivorship. The size of the tenant in common's share is unaffected by the death of any other tenant in common, whose share passes on will or intestacy.

3. Of the four unities only unity of possession is essential.

4. The size of the shares of each tenant in common need not be equal.

5. If all the tenants in common agree a new document can be executed conveying the land to them as joint tenants thereby converting their co-ownership to a joint tenancy.

Creation of joint tenancies and tenancies in common

After 1925 co-ownership almost invariably took effect behind a trust for sale with the legal estate held on a joint tenancy: L.P.A. 1925, ss.1(6), 34(1), 36(2). It was not possible for a tenancy in common of the legal estate to exist. Consequently when dealing with the distinctions between joint tenancies and tenancies in common we were concerned only with the beneficial interests in the property.

The provisions of Trust of Land and Appointment of Trustees Act 1996 do not fundamentally change the principles relating to co-ownership save that the trust for sale of the land is replaced with a trust of land and the doctrine of conversion is abolished so that the beneficiaries interest remains in the land and is not converted to the proceeds of sale.

From 1997 all co-ownership will operate on a mechanism whereby the legal estate will be held by trustees who are always joint tenants on the statutory imposed trust of land. The equitable interests take effect behind the trust either as joint tenants or tenants in common.

Tests for determining the status of the co-ownership in equity

The following tests should be applied in order:

1. The four unities. If one of the unities is absent (other than unity of possession) then a tenancy in common is deemed to exist.

2. The express words of the conveyance: the conveyance may reflect the express intention of the grantor, for example "to A.B.C.D. as joint tenants at law and in equity." Such a statement will normally be conclusive.

3. Are any words of severance used in the grant: are there any words indicating a sharing of the property? Examples would include, "in equal shares," "equally," "amongst." The existence of such words creates a tenancy in common as compared with a joint

tenancy where the parties are not entitled to a share, merely a potential right to the whole. In *Joyce v. Barker Bros* (1980), a conveyance to a husband and wife "in fee simple as beneficial joint tenants in common in equal shares" was held to create a joint tenancy on a matter of construction, in that, where two inconsistent provisions appear in a deed, the first words which create a sensible grant are taken. However, see *Martin v. Martin* (1989) where substantially the same wording created a tenancy in common as the words "in equal shares" provided a controlling context for the word joint.

4. Construction of the document as a whole: this may indicate the grantor's intention, as for example, where there is a gift of several children with a power to advance capital to a child. This indicates that each is to have a share and therefore a tenancy in common arises. In *Re North* (1952), a bequest to A and B on condition that they pay in equal shares £10 per week to X during her lifetime, created a tenancy in common in that the gift was held to correspond to the obligation.

5. Presumptions of equity: there are a variety of situations where equity presumes a tenancy in common. These presumptions only apply where the above tests do not operate.

(a) If the purchase money is provided in unequal shares, a tenancy in common in proportion to the share of the money advanced is presumed: *Bull v. Bull* (1955). If the purchase money is provided in equal shares, a presumption is in favour of a joint tenancy. Either presumption can be displaced by contrary evidence.

(b) If money is advanced on mortgage, whether in equal or unequal shares a tenancy in common is presumed: each means to lend his own and take back his own. Joint account clauses have no effect on the presumption: L.P.A. 1925, s.111.

(c) If land is acquired by partners as part of partnership assets a tenancy in common is presumed: *Lake v. Craddock* (1732). No formal partnership is required, the rule applies to any joint undertaking with a view to profit. The right of survivorship has no place in business.

(d) On the construction of executory trusts, equity leans in favour of a tenancy in common in, for example, gifts to children as a class.

The category of equitable presumptions is not closed: *Malayan Credit Limited v. Jack Chia—M.P.H.* (1986)—rent payable in unequal shares is equivalent to providing the purchase money in unequal shares and therefore a tenancy in common is presumed.

6. Where none of the above tests apply the parties are deemed to be beneficial joint tenants.

EFFECT OF THE 1925 AND 1996 LEGISLATION

1. At law, the only form of co-ownership now permitted is a joint tenancy, mainly because of its relative simplicity for tracing title to land: L.P.A. 1925, ss.34(1), 36(2). A tenancy in common can still exist in equity as before. A joint tenancy at law cannot be converted into a tenancy in common at law.

2. The legal estate is held on a trust of land with the holders of the legal estate acting as trustees on a joint tenancy: L.P.A. 1925, ss.34; 36 as amended, 1996 Act ss.4; 6. The trustees hold the legal estate for the persons entitled in equity on the terms of the trusts which may be express or imposed by statute. The trustees have the powers of an absolute owner of land.

If the trustees exercise their power to sell the land the interests of the beneficiaries are overreached and their interest operates on the purchase money which replaces the land. The doctrine of conversion no longer operates by virtue of 2.3 of the 1996 Act and until sale the interests of the beneficiaries are interests in land.

3. The legal estate is held by the trustees who are no longer under a duty to sell the land, though they have a discretion as to whether a sale should take place. In the event of any dispute between the trustees, s.14 1996 Act provides that any trustee or other person having an interest in land subject to the trust may apply for a court order concerning the land (this effectively replaces s.30 L.P.A. 1925). The trustees must consult with the beneficiaries and give effect to their wishes as far as possible and provided those wishes are consistent with the purposes of the trust of land.

4. The legal estate cannot be vested in more than four persons. Where the conveyance is to the co-owners themselves, the legal estate is vested in up to the first four named in the conveyance who are of full age and capacity and who are willing to act. Consequently the number of trustees cannot be increased beyond four. The following examples serve to illustrate:

    (a) a conveyance to A and B who are of full age and capacity. A and B hold the legal estate as trustees on a statutory trust of land as joint tenants at law for the benefits of themselves as co-owners in equity;

    (b) a similar conveyance to A, B, C, D and E. Here the first four hold the legal estate as trustees for the benefit of all five in equity;

(c) a conveyance to X and Y to hold for the benefit of A, B and
C. Here the trustees have been expressly named and X and
Y hold the legal estate on trust of land for the benefit of A,
B and C as co-owners in equity.

Conversion of a joint tenancy into a tenancy in common

It should at the outset be emphasised that the legal estate must
always be held on a joint tenancy and cannot be severed, *i.e.* converted into a tenancy in common. Severance is only possible in
respect of the beneficial interests of the co-owners. A joint tenancy
can be converted into a tenancy in common in a number of ways.
Generally they depend upon severance of one or more of the
unities.

1. Acquisition of another estate or interest in the land subsequent to the creation of the joint tenancy.

2. Alienation *inter vivos*: Where a joint tenant sells his potential
share the purchaser becomes a tenant in common as to that share
and other joint tenants remain joint tenants as to the rest of the
estate. The alienation may be involuntary, for example, where the
interest in the joint tenancy passes to a trustee in bankruptcy on
an insolvency: *Re Dennis* (1992). Partial alienation by way of mortgage or creating a life interest also severs the joint tenancy.

Where a joint tenant enters into a contract to sell his share or
covenants to settle the property this may amount to an alienation
in equity and is effective to sever the joint tenancy.

3. Homicide: a person cannot benefit from his crime so that if
one joint tenant criminally kills another he cannot take any benefit
by way of survivorship. If A and B hold as joint tenants at law and
in equity and A murders B, A holds the legal estate for himself
and the estate of B as tenants in common in equity: *Schobelt v.
Barber* (1967). If there are three joint tenants A, B and C and A
murders B, A and C hold the legal estate on trust for C as to
one-third on a tenancy in common and A and C as joint tenants
as to two-thirds. There is a constructive trust imposed on A, for
the benefit of C.

4. Notice in writing under L.P.A. 1925, s.36(2): if a joint tenant
desires to sever the joint tenancy he can achieve this by giving the
other joint tenants notice in writing of this desire. A notice which
has been posted but not received is effective: *Re 88 Berkeley Road,
London N.W.9* (1971): *McDowell v. Hirschfield, Lipson & Rumney*
(1992).

In *Re Drapers Conv.* (1969), the issue of a summons by a wife
claiming a sale of the matrimonial home amounted to notice for

this purpose, though in *Harris v. Goddard* (1983), there was no severance where a divorce petition had been served on a husband and a prayer in the petition stated that "such order may be made by way of transfer of settlement of property in respect of the matrimonial home." All the prayer did was invite the court to consider at some future date where to exercise its jurisdiction: see also *Goodman v. Gallant* (1986).

5. By mutual agreement among the joint tenants: even where an agreement is not specifically enforceable between the parties it does not matter provided a common intention to sever is indicated. In *Burgess v. Rawnsley* (1975), an oral agreement by joint tenants whereby one was to buy the share of the other for £750 was held to amount to a severance of the joint tenancy even though the agreement was not enforceable under L.P.A. 1925, s.40. The oral agreement and the conduct of the parties was sufficient evidence to satisfy L.P.A. 1925, s.36(2) as an example of ". . . such other acts or things as would, in the case of personal estate, have been effectual to sever the tenancy in equity." In *Hunter v. Babbage* (1994) the court confirmed that an agreement that was not enforceable could nevertheless operate to sever the joint tenancy as the unenforceable agreement was evidence of a common intention to sever.

6. Courses of conduct or dealing: implicit in the *Burgess v. Rawnsley* decision is that if there is a course of dealing in which one party makes clear to the other that he desires that their shares should no longer be held jointly but be held in common then a severance occurs. Consequently if joint tenants negotiate the rearrangement of their interests, even if their negotiations break down, a severance may result: *cf. Greenfield v. Greenfield* (1979); *Barton v. Morris* (1985): *Gore & Snell v. Carpenter* (1990).

TERMINATION OF CO-OWNERSHIP

1. Partition: this is a mechanism whereby the land is physically divided between the co-owners. The joint tenants must be of full age and partition must normally be effected by deed. On partition each co-owner becomes absolutely entitled to a separate plot of land. Under s.7 of the 1996 Act the trustees of land have powers of partition.

2. Sale of the legal estate: where the trustees comply with the trust of land and transfer title to a purchaser the beneficiaries' interests are overreached and the co-ownership terminates.

3. Union in sole ownership: this may occur where all the legal and beneficial interests are finally vested in one person:

(a) on a survival of the last joint tenant;
(b) release by one joint tenant of his interest to another. Here the sole owner can call for the trustees to transfer the legal title to him: *Cooper v. Critchley* (1955);
(c) where tenants in common leave their interest by will or intestacy to a remaining co-owner.

Single trustee protection—purchasers

Where land subject to co-ownership is sold the purchaser should normally transfer the purchase money to at least two trustees. However, where there is a sole survivor in law and equity a purchaser is protected and will obtain good title if he pays the proceeds of sale to the single trustee. This is because of the provisions of the Law of Property (Joint Tenants) Act 1964, as amended by the Law of Property (Miscellaneous Provisions) Act 1994 which provides that the survivor of a joint tenancy can pass good title to a purchaser free from any equitable interest created by a severance, unless a memorandum of severance has been indorsed on or annexed to the conveyance vesting the legal estate in the joint tenants.

The protection of the 1964 Act as amended does not apply if the land is registered: s.3 1964 Act.

Sale of trust land; powers of trustees; consultation

As previously indicated in Chapter 6 the effect of the 1996 Act on this aspect of co-ownership is significant. Currently in a co-ownership situation a trust of land is created. There is no trust for sale but the trustees have wide powers of sale should they choose to exercise them. If the trustees cannot agree as to whether the land should be sold, they, or any interested party, may apply to the court for it to make such order as it thinks fit: s.14 1996 Act replacing s.30 L.P.A. 1925.

If trustees choose to exercise the power to sell they have all the powers of an absolute owner. On a sale the proceeds are held for the beneficiaries whose interests in the land becomes overreached. The doctrine of conversion is no longer operational.

Before exercising any power of sale the trustees must obtain any consents required by the instrument creating the trust of land and consultation with the beneficiaries has been extended. After consultation the trustees should give effect to the wishes of the beneficiaries calculated by value, provided this is not inconsistent with the purposes of the trust. These provisions replace s.26(3) L.P.A. 1925.

If no solution to disagreement between trustees can be found an order of the court may be necessary.

The court's discretion under s.14 will be exercised in much the same way as it was under s.30 L.P.A. 1925 and the pre-1997 case law will be relied upon to give guidance. One point of difference in considering whether any sale should take place is that under the s.30 cases a trust for sale was the norm whereas under s.14 there is a power of sale with no imperative direction. In exercising any discretion the courts will take into account that many trusts are created for a particular purpose and refuse a sale where to allow it to take place would defeat that original purpose. It may be wrong for one of the parties to the trust to try to enforce a sale in order to defeat one of its objects. In *Re Buchanan-Wollaston's Conveyance* (1939), there were four owners of property, each neighbouring but separate, who combined to buy a piece of land which they desired to keep as an open space. The land was conveyed to them as joint tenants and a statutory trust for sale arose. The parties entered into a covenant in which they agreed to preserve the open space. One party sold his property and then applied to have the communal property sold. The court refused a sale on a section 30 application as they would not allow a man in breach of his obligation to prevail. See also *Barclay v. Barclay* (1970). Where the purpose behind the trust for sale is to provide a matrimonial home, then so long as the marriage is still alive, the court will not allow an arbitrary sale of the property: *Jones v. Challenger* (1961), though if the parties are divorced, and the purpose no longer prevails, the trust may take effect: *Bedson v. Bedson* (1965). In matrimonial cases, the subsistence of the marriage is a crucial factor, though the courts always take into account the wider circumstances of the case and in particular the requirements of the children, the parties' conduct, the financial circumstances of the parties and their contribution to the acquisition of the property.

Section 14 emphasises factors such as the intentions of the persons who established the trust, the purposes for which the property is held, the welfare of any child who occupies the land as his home, the interests of any secured creditor and where appropriate the wishes of the beneficiaries. The courts will consider special factors where the dispute concerning sale arises from an application made by a trustee in bankruptcy: s.335A Insolvency Act 1996.

Co-ownership and the matrimonial home

1. A spouse has a right of occupation in the matrimonial home under the Matrimonial Homes Act 1982. The rights granted are

registrable as Class F landcharge under the L.C.A. 1972 or can be protected by a notice under the L.R.A. 1925. Such rights do not constitute overriding interests in respect of registered land. As to the effects of registration: *Kashmir Kaur v. Gill* (1988).

2. Where a spouse makes a substantial contribution in money or money's worth to the improvement of the home in which either or both of them have a beneficial interest, then a beneficial share is created with the courts will quantify according to what seems just in all the circumstances: Matrimonial Proceedings and Property Act 1970, s.37. This is independent of any interest granted under general equitable principles.

3. Under the Matrimonial Causes Act 1973, on the breakdown of a marriage the court has wide discretionary powers to order a distribution of the spouses' property.

4. Once the Family Law Act 1996 Part IV is fully implemented a rationalisation of the spouse's rights of occupation of the matrimonial home and principles governing matrimonial property will take place. However, criticism and opposition to some of these proposals may result in a watering down and delay in their operation.

CO-OWNERSHIP AND TRUSTS

If land is held in the name of one person, but the purchase price was provided by more than one person this may give rise to the courts imposing a trust. Traditionally, the courts distinguished between resulting and constructive trusts, however, in recent decisions the categories seem to have been merged and wherever a trust is imposed by the courts other than via an express declaration it is termed a constructive trust. If it can be inferred that there was a "common intention" by the parties that the person not named on the title would acquire an interest by virtue of his or her contribution then a constructive trust may be imposed: *Lloyds Bank v. Rossett* (1990). Where, there is sufficient evidence to infer the requisite common intention to share and the consequent detrimental reliance thereon then the task of the court is to quantify the size of the respective shares, which can be a difficult task: *Stokes v. Anderson* (1991).

1. Establishing a common intention is often problematical and is a matter of inference from the conduct of the parties: *Grant v. Edwards* (1986); *Thomas v. Fuller-Brown* (1988).

2. If there is an arrangement, agreement or understanding between the parties that the property is to be shared beneficially,

the court may infer a constructive trust if the claimant can show a detrimental reliance.

3. It was held in *Gissing v. Gissing* (1971) that indirect financial contributions did not give rise to a beneficial interest, though this was questioned in *Hazel v. Hazel* (1972) and *Grant v. Edwards* (1986), where it was held that contributions to household expenses gave rise to a beneficial interest.

4. The courts may find an equitable solution to the contribution cases through the principle of estoppel, as there seems to be an overlapping of principle with the constructive trust cases: *Eves v. Eves* (1975). Where the courts are satisfied that there has been a prior agreement and a contribution by a beneficial claimant the court is also concerned as to the size of the share of the beneficiary: *Midland Bank v. Cooke* (1995).

The position of a purchaser—protection of an interest

Unregistered land

The nature of the equitable interest created under a constructive trust is such that it is not registrable and consequently will be subject to the overreaching machinery, provided the conveyance is made by at least two trustees: sections 2, 27 of L.P.A. 1925. In the case of single owners, overreaching does not apply and the situation is governed by the doctrine of notice.

There has been much dispute as to whether a purchaser of unregistered land has notice of the rights of a spouse of the estate owner, where that spouse lives in the same property. In *Caunce v. Caunce* (1969), the presence of a wife in the matrimonial home was not deemed to constitute notice to the purchaser. This rule was criticised in *Williams & Glyn's Bank Ltd v. Boland* (1981) and *Kingsnorth v. Tizard* (1986) and the better view at present is that a wife's presence is separate from that of her husband and her occupation in the property is deemed to be constructive notice to the purchaser.

Registered land

The interest of a co-owner in actual occupation of the matrimonial home maybe an overriding interest under section $70(1)(g)$ of L.R.A. 1925, unless it has been protected as a minor interest by way of entry of a notice or caution: *Williams & Glyn's Bank Ltd v. Boland* (1981), where a husband held the matrimonial home on trust for sale for himself and his wife. The husband mortgaged the house to a bank. The husband defaulted on the mortgage to the bank and they sought to take possession prior to selling the property. It was held by the House of Lords that the wife had an overriding interest under section 70(1)(g) of L.R.A. 1925 and this bound the bank.

The decision in *Boland* has been qualified in recent decisions:

1. Where the purchase price is paid to at least two trustees, the overreaching provisions operate to allow the purchaser to take free of the beneficial interests: *City of London B.S. v. Flegg* (1988).

2. A beneficial co-owner is deemed to impliedly consent to his rights being subject to those of a mortgagee where he knows that the purchase money has been raised on mortgage: *Paddington B.S. v. Mendelsohn* (1985); *Bristol & West B.S. v. Henning* (1985)—unregistered land. Once consent to the mortgage is given or implied, it is irrelevant that the size of the mortgage is greater than that required: *Abbey National B.S. v. Cann* (1990). In the event of a remortgage by the legal owner, a beneficial co-owner who consents to the original mortgage but has no knowledge of the re-mortgage will be bound by the re-mortgage only to the extent of the value of the original mortgage: *Equity & Law Home Loans Ltd v. Prestridge* (1992). Somewhat surprisingly the court in *Woolwich B.S. v. Dickman* (1996) suggested that a consent by an equitable owner in actual occupation will not assist a purchaser unless the consents are "expressed on the register".

3. The date for determining actual occupation is the date of completion even though registration may not as yet have been completed: *Abbey National B.S. v. Cann* (1990).

8. EASEMENTS AND PROFITS

Introduction

Easements and profits, known collectively as servitudes, are rights annexed to land entitling its owner (the dominant owner) to do, or prevent the doing of, something on another piece of land (the servient tenement). Examples of common easements would include rights of way; light; support and water. A *profit à prendre* is a right to enter another's land and take something from the land which is the natural produce of the soil.

1. An easement may be either positive or negative: a positive easement is the right to do something on the land of another, for

example, a right of way, whereas a negative easement imposes a restriction such as with a right of light, where the servient owner may not build so as unreasonably to obstruct the flow of light. Similarly a right of support imposes a restriction that a neighbour's property will not be disturbed.

2. The nature of an easement is such that it does not vest a proprietory or possessory right in the owner of the dominant tenement: In *Copeland v. Greenhalf* (1952), the use of a stretch of roadway for storage of vehicles and wheels did not amount to an easement in that the claim really amounted to a claim of joint user (proprietory) and was too wide and ill defined in nature as to constitute an easement: *Pavledes v. Ryesbridge Properties Ltd* (1989).

3. An easement can be a legal interest in land, provided it is created by statute, deed or prescription and it complies with L.P.A. 1925, s.1(2)(*a*), *i.e.* "an easement right or privilege in or over land for an interest equivalent to an estate in fee simple absolute in possession or term of years absolute". If legal, the right can be enforced against anybody who comes to the land, irrespective of notice. Any other easement is necessarily equitable.

4. At common law the benefit of an easement passes with the transfer of the land to which it is annexed without being specially mentioned and by virtue of L.P.A. 1925, s.62(1) it is provided that "a conveyance . . . shall operate to convey with the land all . . . easements, rights and advantages whatsoever . . ." provided such rights relate to the land and no contrary intention is expressed in the conveyance.

Essentials of an easement

It was laid down in *Re Ellenborough Park* (1956), that there are four essentials for an easement to exist.

1. There must be a dominant and servient tenement: An easement must be connected to land and not merely be personal in nature, *i.e.* no easement can exist "in gross"—independent of ownership in land. A privilege to a person with no dominant land is a licence.

    (a) An easement can be acquired even if the dominant owner is a lessee only: *Thorp v. Brummitt* (1873).

    (b) The court will determine the extent of land capable of benefitting: *Callard v. Beeney* (1930).

    (c) An easement cannot exist unless and until there was both a dominant and a servient tenement in separate ownership: *London and Blenham Estates Ltd v. Ladbroke Retail Parks Ltd* (1993)—no easement existed because the potential servient

tenement had been transferred before the dominant tenement had been acquired.

2. The easement must accommodate the dominant tenement:
An easement must confer a benefit on the dominant tenement, it
"must have some natural connection with the estate as being for
its benefit": *per* Byles J. in *Bailey v. Stephens* (1862). The test is does
it make the dominant tenement a better and more convenient
property, *i.e.* it is necessary to show a nexus between the user of
the dominant tenement and the enjoyment of the right. This may
be established by showing that the general utility of the dominant
tenement has been improved or by giving a means of access or light
and also by benefitting some trade, particularly if that trade is long
established. In *Moody v. Steggles* (1879), it was held that the right
to fix an advertising signboard to an adjoining property accommod-
ated a public house.

   (a) Although the dominant and servient tenement need not be
       adjoining, they must be sufficiently proximate for a practical
       benefit to be conferred. "You cannot have a right of way over
       land in Kent appurtenant to an estate in London." *per* Byles
       J., *Bailey v. Stephens* (1862), though this is not an absolute
       test in that a signboard attached to a property adjoining a
       motorway and advertising holiday flatlets at a resort hun-
       dreds of miles away might accommodate the dominant tene-
       ment. In *Re Ellenborough Park* (1956) itself, a *jus spatiandi*
       (right of perambulation) to use a park was held to benefit not
       only houses fronting the park but also houses neighbouring
       though not themselves adjacent.

   (b) Where a right is granted to exploit an independent business
       enterprise this may amount only to a licence, as in *Hill v.
       Tupper* (1863) where a grant by a canal company of the "sole
       and exclusive right . . . to put or use boats on the said canal
       . . ." amounted only to a mere personal licence as it did not
       exist for the purpose of the land as such.

3. The dominant and servient tenement must not be owned and
occupied by the same person: Rights exercised by an owner over
other land of his own are known as quasi-easements. Such
easements do not necessarily pass to the purchaser of the
quasi-dominant tenement without express mention.

4. The easement must be capable of forming the subject-matter
of a grant:

   (a) There must be a capable grantor and grantee: A problem
       can arise where a tenement is owned by a corporation

which may not have the power to grant or receive easements.

(b) The rights must be within the general nature of rights capable of existing as easements: Although the list of easements is not closed and as stated in *Dyce v. Hay* (1852) must expand with the changes that take place in the circumstances of mankind, it nevertheless follows that "incidents of a novel kind cannot be devised at the fancy or caprice of any owner"; *Keppel v. Bailey* (1834). New easements have from time to time been recognised.

Examples include:

  (i) the right to park a motor vehicle in a defined area; *Newman v. Jones* (1982); *London and Blenham Estates Ltd v. Ladbroke Retail Parks Ltd* (1993). It will not be a valid objection to the existence of such easement that charges are made whether for the parking itself or for the general upkeep of the park;

  (ii) the right to use an airfield; *Dowty Boulton Paul Ltd v. Wolverhampton Corp. (No. 2)* (1976);

  (iii) the right to the passage of piped water across another person's land; *Rance v. Elvin* (1985);

  (iv) the right to require the servient owner to fence his land; *Crow v. Wood* (1971).

It is not necessary that new easements should be within one of the recognised categories (way, water, light, support) provided the right satisfies the four general characteristics of an easement. A right which has caused difficulties over the years is the right to store goods. The right was regarded as being capable of existing as an easement in *Att.-Gen. for S. Nigeria v. Holt* (1915)—the right to store casks and trade produce in a warehouse; and in *Wright v. Macadam* (1949)—the right to store coal in a coal bunker. Conversely it was established in *Copeland v. Greenhalf* (1952) and more recently in *Grigsby v. Melville* (1974)—right to store in an adjoining cellar; that where the right is tantamount to a grant of joint or exclusive user of the servient tenement, this is too extensive to be capable of constituting an easement.

(c) The right must be sufficiently defined: A vague or inexact right cannot exist as an easement. There is no easement of privacy: *Browne v. Flower* (1911), or the right to a view, or of a general flow of air (not in a defined channel) over land: *Harris v. Pinna* (1886).

CREATION OF EASEMENTS

As a basic principle all easements must have their origin in a grant and most methods of acquisition are traceable to an express or implied grant. The following methods of acquisition exist:

1. Statute

Easements may be granted by local Acts of Parliament, for example, giving a right of support to a canal constructed under statute or by general Act of Parliament, giving rights in respect of cables, gas pipes, sewers, etc.

2. Express grant or reservation

A common way of creating easements is by way of express grant by deed. This is effective at common law and the terms of the grant will govern its extent of use in the future: *Jelbert v. Davis* (1968).

(a) In equity, if a grantee under an informal grant materially alters his position (for example, by spending money) and the grantor acquiesces, the grantee will have an easement in equity: *McManus v. Cooke* (1887)—rebuilding a party wall. A contract for the creation of an easement that satisfies s.2 Law of Property (Miscellaneous Provisions) Act 1989 and is specifically enforceable under the *Walsh v. Lonsdale* (1882) rule will create a valid equitable easement. *Cf. Thatcher v. Douglas* (1996)—oral contracts will not be enforceable.

(b) Where a landowner sells off part of his land he may expressly reserve certain easements or profits for use of the part sold. A simple reservation was not possible before 1926, but now by virtue of L.P.A. 1925, s.65, an express reservation by deed is effective and no regrant is necessary.

(c) Under L.P.A. 1925, s.62 subject to a contrary intention expressed in the conveyance, every *conveyance* of land passes all privileges, easements, rights and advantages appertaining or reputed to appertain to the land or part of it. Thus, a conveyance may include a right of way over other property even if not expressly mentioned in the conveyance.

    (i) The section may operate to convert informal rights into valid easements: *Wright v. Macadam* (1940)—the permissive right to use a coal bunker passed under section 62 on the grant of a new lease.

    (ii) The term "conveyance" does not include an oral lease or a contract for a lease: L.P.A., s.205(i)(ii); *Borman v. Griffith* (1930).

(iii) Section 62 does not apply where occupation and owner-ship are not severed immediately prior to the convey-ance, *i.e.* section 62 does not apply to quasi-easements: *Sovmots Inv. Ltd v. Secretary of State for the Environment* (1979) though easements of light may be an exception: *Broomfield v. Williams* (1897).

(iv) The section will only apply where the right is capable of being granted at law: *Green v. Ascho Horticulturalist Ltd* (1966).

3. Implied grant

This relates to quasi-easements, *i.e.* rights exercised by an owner over his own land. On a severance, whether by conveyance, lease, or devise, quasi-easements may become easements in favour of either party (originally based on the presumed common intention of the parties). Three situations must be considered:

(a) Sale of the quasi-servient tenement. As a general rule a grant is construed against the grantor and few easements are implied in favour of the grantor. The attitude of the courts being that if the quasi-servient owner desires to reserve any easements he should do so expressly. The only implied easements which form an exception to the rule are:

  (i) rights of support for buildings;

  (ii) rights of way of necessity of a land locked close which has been retained. *N.B. Barry v. Haseldine* (1952)—a right of way of necessity could exist even though the quasi-dominant tenement is not entirely surrounded by the quasi-servient tenement and even if a permissive right of access is available from a third party at the time of conveyance: *London Corp. v. Riggs* (1880)—the extent of a right of way of necessity is restricted to the mode of enjoyment of the quasi-dominant tenement at the time of the grant. It may not be used for additional purposes connected with a change in user of the land. In *Nickerson v. Barraclough* (1980), the Court of Appeal specified that the basis of a right of way of necessity was founded on the intention of the parties and the implications from the circumstances and not the public policy principles that land should not be made unusable and a grantor cannot derogate from his grant: *M.R.A. Engineering Ltd v. Trimster Company Ltd* (1988). In *Manjang v. Drammah* (1991), the Privy Council confirmed that an available access by water, even though less convenient than access across land, was sufficient to negative any implication of a right of way of necessity.

   (iii) any easement which gives effect to the presumed common intention of the parties or situations which preclude a grantee from denying the right consistently with good faith: *Re Webb's Lease* (1951).

(b) Sale of the quasi-dominant tenement; The law is more inclined to imply easements in favour of the grantee in this situation and the following implied easements will prevail.

   (i) Those easements which pass under the rule in *Wheeldon v. Burrows* (1878), which provides that a grant of the quasi-dominant tenement will pass "all those continuous and apparent ... quasi-easement ... which are necessary to the reasonable enjoyment of the property granted and were actually enjoyed prior to the conveyance". "Continuous" appears to mean permanent, and together with "apparent" implies that the right leaves an obvious and permanent mark on the land itself or at least one revealed by a careful inspection. A rough trackway was sufficient in *Hansford v. Jago* (1921). Other examples would include water flowing through visible pipes, windows enjoying light or a defined passageway. It has never been clearly established whether the reference to the right being reasonably necessary to the enjoyment of the land is an alternative to the right being continuous and apparent or whether both must be satisfied. In *Wheeler v. J.J. Saunders* (1995) a right of way was held not to be necessary for the reasonable enjoyment of the land because an alternative access to the property existed.

   (ii) Easements which give effect to the presumed common intention of the parties, even if neither party had actually considered the matter at the time of the grant: *Wong v. Beaumont Property Trust Ltd* (1965).

   (iii) Easements of necessity together with any ancillary easements.

In comparing the operation of L.P.A. 1925, s.62 with the rule in *Wheeldon v. Burrows* (1978), it can be observed that section 62 does not apply to quasi-easements, nor does it apply where there is no "conveyance" within L.P.A. 1925, s.205(i)(ii). See *Borman v. Griffith* (1930). However, section 62 may convey easements to which the grantee has no contractual rights.

(c) Sale of two plots in common ownership:

(i) Contemporaneous sale: the effect is as if the owner had sold the dominant tenement and retained the rest: *Schwann v. Cotton* (1916).

(ii) Separate sales: the second purchaser is in the same position as the vendor, so that if the quasi-servient tenement is sold first, only easements of necessity, support and those which give effect to presumed intention will be reserved and the purchaser from him will be in no better position: *White v. Taylor* (1968).

4. Presumed grant

This applies to easements acquired by prescription, where the law presumes from long enjoyment that the right had a lawful origin in a grant. A prescriptive right may be acquired at common law, under the doctrine of lost modern grant or under the Prescription Act 1832. In each case the following common criteria must be established:

(a) The use is "as of right." This is explained in the maxim *nec per vim, nec clam, nec precario*, which requires that the right has not been obtained by force or coercion, and that it is not secretive: *Union Lighterage Co. v. London Growing Dock Co.* (1902), nor is it permissive in nature: *Gardner v. Hodson's Kingston Brewery* (1903); *Healey v. Hawkins* (1968). In *Mills v. Silver* (1990), a prescriptive right to use a track was claimed. Successive owners had allowed usage of the track because of good neighbourliness and because usage had previously been regarded as insignificant. Nevertheless, the court held that there had been acquiescence in the use of the track, permission had never been sought and consequently the right had been established. In *Bridle v. Ruby* (1988) mistaken belief that a right of way had been legally acquired did not prevent a 22 year user becoming a right by prescription since it was still deemed "as of right". In *Jones v. Price* (1992) it was held that there was no prescriptive easement even though a trackway had been used from 1926 to 1979 since the right to use the trackway was acquired with permission and continued by tacit consent until permission was withdrawn in 1979.

(b) The user must be continuous, as far as the nature of the right allows. User can be by successive owners of the dominant tenement: *Davis v. Whitby* (1974). A right of way used precariously (blocked at irregular intervals) could not develop into an easement: *Goldsmith and another v. Burrow Construction Co. Ltd and another* (1987).

(c) The user must be by or on behalf of a fee simple owner against a fee simple owner. If a tenant acquires an easement against a third party he acquires it on behalf of the fee simple estate. If a tenant occupies the servient tenement, an easement cannot be acquired against it, though if user began against a fee simple owner, it does not make it invalid for prescriptive purposes if the land is later leased. Easements cannot be prescribed for by one tenant against another tenant of the same landlord: *Simmons v. Dobson* (1991).

Common law prescription

At common law a grant was presumed if enjoyment dated from "time immemorial," *i.e.* 1189. This was converted into the test of living memory and in recent times a user of twenty years or more has sufficed. Such grant would not be available if at any time since 1189 the right could not have existed, for example, a claim to a right of light to a building erected after that date would fail.

Lost modern grant

A mechanism to avoid the rigours of the common law rule was developed by the courts under the fiction of lost modern grant. If a claimant can show actual enjoyment for a reasonable period, the court is bound to presume an actual grant which was later lost. Twenty years or more may be sufficient for this purpose though the cases establish that 40 years is more usual. The claim may be defeated if proof is given that during the entire period since user started there has been no person capable of granting easements: *Tehidy Minerals Ltd v. Norman* (1971). Even though most claims will fall under the Prescription Act 1832 the doctrine of lost modern grant may still be used: *Re St Martin-Le-Grand, York* (1989); *Mills v. Silver* (1990).

Prescription Act 1832

The object of the Act was to simplify the method of acquisition of easements by prescription, but what in fact resulted was one of the most badly drafted statutes on record. The Act treats easements of light differently from other easements.

Easements other than light. Section 2 provides that an easement can be claimed where it is "actually enjoyed by any person claiming right thereto without interruption for the full period of 20 years" and it shall not be defeated by showing that the user began at any time prior to the 20 year period, though it may still be defeated in other ways (for example, that it was secretive, permissive or forceable).

Actual enjoyment for 40 years makes the right "absolute and indefeasible" unless enjoyed by express consent given by deed or writing.

(a) In each case the period of years is the period immediately preceding some "suit or action wherein the claim … shall be brought into question," *i.e.* an action by the parties relating to trespass or nuisance or merely an application for a declaration: section 4.

(b) The period must be uninterrupted, and to constitute an interruption, there must be some act which shows the easement is disputed which lasts for a year and which has been "submitted to or acquiesced in" by the dominant owner. Enjoyment for 19 years and one day may suffice if the dominant owner takes court action on the first day of the twenty-first year, provided the servient owner has not taken court action previously. Consequently any interruption may only have lasted for 364 days, which is less than a year and will not count: *Reilly v. Orange* (1955). Where the dominant owner protests at the existence of an interruption, this appears to postpone the commencement of that interruption for a reasonable period of time: *Davies v. Du Paver* (1953). Where the servient owner lodges a complaint with the dominant owner about the existence of a right this may amount to an interruption. If the dominant owner then fails to communicate with the servient owner after the complaint has been made then this will be construed as a "submission or acquiescence" to the interruption: *Dance v. Triplow* (1992).

(c) The term "claiming right thereto" appears to mean the same as "as or right."

(d) Any form of permission (written or oral) will defeat the 20 year period, though an oral permission given before the 40 year period started can be ignored and will not defeat the claim.

(e) Certain periods of disability must be deducted from the 20 and 40 year claims: see ss.7 and 8.

Easements of light. Section 3 provides that where a right of light has been actually enjoyed for a full period of 20 years without interruption the right becomes absolute and indefeasible, unless enjoyed by written consent or agreement. Oral permission will not defeat this claim even if "rent" is paid.

(a) The amount of light that a building is entitled to is that which is required for any ordinary purpose for which the building has been constructed or adapted: *Colls v. Home and Colonial Stores Ltd* (1904); *Allen v. Greenwood* (1979).

(b) An interruption of a right of light may be effected by erecting an obstruction, or alternatively by registration of a local land charge to have effect as an obstruction under the Rights of Light Act 1959.

(c) A fee simple owner is bound by an easement of light acquired by a third party when the land was in the occupation of a tenant.

(d) One tenant may acquire an easement of light against another tenant of the same landlord.

(e) The disabilities under section 7 of the Act do not apply to easements of light.

Protection of easement against third parties

In unregistered land an equitable easement can be registered as a class D(iii) land charge. If not registered it will not be binding on a purchaser of a legal estate for money or money's worth. A legal easement is a right *in rem* and binds the whole world. In *Ives v. High* (1967), an easement created by estoppel was held not to be a registrable interest under the Land Charges Act. Its enforceability depended on the pre-1926 doctrine of notice. In registered land, as a consequence of the decisions in *Celsteel v. Alton House Holdings* (1985); *Thatcher v. Douglas* (1996), an equitable easement may constitute an overriding interest under Land Registration Act, s.70(*1*)(*a*), which also covers other easements. Note also s.70(1)(*g*).

Extinguishment of easements

1. Release.

(a) express—a deed is essential at common law, but equity will assist a servient owner who, relying on an agreement to release, prejudices his position;

(b) implied—an intention to abandon must be shown, but non-user by itself is not conclusive. Alteration of the dominant tenement may imply the necessary intention: *Swan v. Sinclair* (1924). Non-user for 175 years of a grant of a right of way made in 1818 did not of itself indicate an intention to abandon it: *Benn v. Hardinge* (1992).

(c) change of circumstance—it may be possible for an easement to be extinguished where circumstances are such that there is no longer any practical possibility of the easement ever again benefitting the dominant tenement in the manner contemplated in the grant: *Huckvale and Another v. Aegean Hotels Ltd* (1989).

2. Unity of seisin. Where the fee simple and possession in both plots of land come into the same hands this will extinguish the easement, which does not revive on subsequent severence of the plots.

3. Statute. As under the Commons Registration Act 1965.

Profits à prendre

1. Nature: A profit is a right to take something off another person's land but it is confined to parts of the land, for example, minerals, crops, or wild animals. The thing taken must at the time be capable of ownership. A profit can be distinguished from an easement in the following ways:

(a) a profit can be granted "in gross," *i.e.* independent of ownership of land. A profit in gross may be acquired by prescription at common law: *Lovett and Another v. Fairclough and Others* (1990);

(b) the owner of a profit enjoys possessory rights over the servient tenement, and may sue in trespass;

(c) an indefinite and fluctuating class of persons cannot acquire a profit as the land would become exhausted;

(d) a profit may be "appendant," *i.e.* annexed to land by operation of law, but if it is "appurtenant" it must satisfy the same rules as easements and is limited to the requirements of the dominant tenement;

(e) profits are overriding interests under section 70(1)(*a*) of the Land Registration Act 1925, whether legal or equitable.

2. Classification: Profits may be classified according to ownership, in relation to land, or by way of subject-matter.

(a) As to ownership:

    (i) a "several" profit is enjoyed by one person to the exclusion of all others;

    (ii) a profit "in common" is enjoyed in common with others.

(b) In relation to land:

    (i) a profit "appurtenant" is annexed to the dominant tenement;

    (ii) a profit "appendant" is annexed to land by operation

of law, for example, an automatic grant of pasture for animals needed to plough arable land granted by the lord;

   (iii) a profit *pur cause de vicinage* applies only to commons of pasture if two adjoining commons allow cattle to stray from one to the other;

(c) By subject-matter:

   (i) profit of pasture: This may exist in all four forms discussed above;

   (ii) profit of turbory: the right to take peat or turf for fuel;

   (iii) profit for estovers: to take wood for hay, house or plough-bote;

   (iv) profit of piscary: to take fish;

   (v) profit in the soil: to take sand, stone, gravel, etc.

Acquisition and extinguishment of profits

In general these are similar to easements, though the implied grant (*Wheeldon v. Burrows* (1878)) cannot apply and the periods under the Prescription Act 1832 are 30 and 60 years respectively, subject to the slight amendments under the Commons Registration Act 1965, s.16.

Access to Neighbouring Land Act (1992)

There is no general common law right to enter a neighbour's land, *e.g.* to conduct repairs on your own property, though this right may exist as an easement. A significant change in the law occurred in 1992 under the Access to Neighbouring Land Act 1992. The Act makes provision to enable a person to gain access, by obtaining an "access order" from the court, to neighbouring land in order to carry out works which are reasonably necessary for the preservation of his own land. An access order will be binding on the successors in title of the servient land if protected on the register prior to the transfer of that land. Although not necessary, an applicant can protect an access order by entering a caution on the register. In unregistered land an access order should be registered in the registry of writs and orders affecting land.

9. MORTGAGES

Definition

1. A mortgage is a conveyance or disposition of land or other property as security for the payment of money or the discharge of some other obligation subject to the right to redeem, *i.e.* that the land or other property has to be retransferred if the money is repaid or the obligation performed.

2. The person who borrows the money is known as the *mortgagor* and the lender is the *mortgagee*.

3. The mortgagee acquires a real rather than a personal security which prevails against other creditors on, for example, the mortgagor's bankruptcy.

CREATION OF MORTGAGES

Prior to 1926 a mortgage of freehold property was created by a conveyance of the fee simple in the land to the mortgagee subject to a covenant to reconvey the land when the debt was repaid. Consequently it was normal for only one legal mortgage to be created. Mortgages of leaseholds were created either by assigning the lease subject to a provision for redemption or by the mortgagor creating a sub-lease with a similar proviso for redemption.

Legal mortgages

1. Mortgages of a fee simple estate must, since 1926, be created in one of two ways: L.P.A. 1925, s.85(1).
   (a) by a demise for a term of years absolute, subject to a provision for redemption; or
   (b) by a charge by deed expressed to be by way of legal mortgage.

2. Legal mortgages of a term of years absolute can be created in two ways; L.P.A. 1925, s.86(1):
   (a) by granting a sub-lease of a term of years absolute to the mortgagee subject to a provision for redemption; or
   (b) by a charge by deed expressed to be by way of legal mortgage.

3. Where a charge is used the mortgagee has all the same protection, powers and remedies as if the mortgage had been created by the grant of a term of years: L.P.A. 1925, s.87(1). The legal chargee does not obtain a legal estate as his security but acquires a legal interest under the L.P.A. 1925, s.1(2)(*c*).

4. A legal charge has some practical advantages over a mortgage created by demise or sub-lease:

(a) it is convenient for mortgaging, for example, a fee simple and a lease together;

(b) it does not infringe a provision (in a lease) against subletting;

(c) the form is shorter and simpler.

Equitable mortgages

A legal mortgage can only be created in respect of a legal estate; however, an owner of a legal estate is still free to create an equitable mortgage over his land by way of security. Equitable mortgages can thereby be created in respect of the legal estate or of an equitable interest itself. Such equitable mortgages can be created in the following ways:

(a) by a deposit of title deeds of land or the land certificate: prior to the coming into force of the L.P. (Miscellaneous Provisions) Act on September 27, 1989, a deposit of title deeds created an equitable mortgage provided it could be shown that the land was intended as security for a loan. If the borrower signed a contemporaneous memorandum under seal, the transaction gave the equitable mortgagee all the powers given by the L.P.A. 1925, including a power of sale. However, the formalities required by the 1989 Act prevents this informal method of creating mortgages as was clearly indicated in *United Bank of Kuwait v. Sahib* (1996). This may not have been the intention of the Act but nevertheless it would appear to apply. The only possible method of saving such mortgages would be to apply the doctrine of estoppel by treating the deposit of title deeds as a promise by the mortgagor which had been acted upon by the mortgagee by the provision of the loan;

(b) a formal agreement to create a legal mortgage: this must now comply with section 2 of the Law of Property (Miscellaneous Provisions) Act 1989. An imperfect legal mortgage can take effect as an agreement, by analogy with L.P.A. 1925, s.40 and the doctrine in *Walsh v. Lonsdale* (1882), subject to the effects of section 2 of the 1989 Act.

(c) mortgage of an equitable interest: this is unaffected by the 1925 legislation and will normally be created by a transfer of the whole interest with a proviso for a retransfer, such transfer to be in writing and signed by the mortgagor: L.P.A. 1925, s.53(1)(c), unless made by will. Written notice to the trustees of the legal estate is advisable where such mortgage is created: L.P.A. 1925, s.137(1).

(d) an equitable charge: this involves appropriating property to the discharge of some obligation without any change in ownership, either at law or in equity.

RIGHTS OF THE MORTGAGOR

The right to redeem

Once a mortgage has been created, there will normally be a contractual date set for repayment of the loan; this is known as the *legal redemption date*. The date is often set six months from the date of the loan, so that the mortgagee's powers can arise. At common law if the money was not paid on the precise date, the property vested in the mortgagee. This was often unfair and so equity intervened and created an *equitable right to redeem, i.e.* it gave the mortgagor the right to redeem the property even after the legal redemption date had passed. This equitable right to redeem should not be confused with the mortgagor's *equity of redemption* which is the sum total of all rights given in equity. It is an interest in land which arises as soon as the mortgage is made and can be sold, leased, etc.

Exclusion of the right to redeem

1. The right to redeem is inviolable and shall not be interfered with. Any provision preventing a mortgagor from recovering his property after performance of his obligation is repugnant to the nature of the transaction and therefore void. This is illustrated in the maxims of equity "once a mortgage always a mortgage": *Seton v. Slade* (1802) and there shall be "no clog or fetter on the right to redeem." A provision in a mortgage that stipulates that property shall belong to the mortgagee on the occurrence of some event is ineffective.

2. Any option to purchase contained in a mortgage is void: *Samual v. Jarrah Timber and Wood Paving Corp. Ltd* (1904). Such is repugnant to the equitable right to redeem even if not oppressive. Once a mortgage has been made any separate and independent transaction giving an option to purchase may be valid: *Reeve v. Lisle* (1902).

Postponement of the right to redeem

1. A provision postponing the date of redemption may be valid provided that the mortgage as a whole is not so oppressive and unconscionable that equity would not enforce it and provided it does not make the equitable right to redeem of no value. In *Fairclough v. Swan Brewery Co. Ltd* (1912), a lease of seventeen-and-a-half years was mortgaged on conditions which prevented its redemption

until six weeks before the end of the term. This was held to make the equitable right to redeem illusory and therefore void. In contrast the House of Lords in *Knightsbridge Estates Trust Ltd v. Byrne* (1939) held that a clause postponing redemption for 40 years was valid and binding, one of the most important reasons being that the parties were large commercial companies who had entered into a mutually enforceable agreement after being professionally advised.

2. A mortgage is subject to the common law rule that any contract in restraint of trade which places an unreasonable restriction upon the freedom of a man to pursue his trade or profession is invalid. A postponement of the right to redeem which is not in itself oppressive may nevertheless become so if accompanied by an excessive restraint upon the mortgagor's activities: *Esso Petroleum v. Harper's Garage* (1968): a 21-year solus agreement was deemed to be unreasonable and oppressive, though a similar agreement for four-and-a-half years was valid. In contrast in *Alec Lobb (Garages) Ltd v. Total Oil (Great Britain) Ltd* (1985), a leaseback agreement of supplies for 21 years was not void as an unreasonable restraint of trade. In *Cleveland Petroleum Co. Ltd v. Dartstone Ltd* (1969) the court distinguished between whether the mortgagor is already in possession and is surrendering a freedom and where the mortgagor is obtaining the property after the solus agreement has been made.

Collateral advantages

1. Sometimes in addition to a mortgagee requiring repayment of the loan and interest he may require some other advantage not inherent in the nature of the mortgage itself. Such clauses are termed "collateral advantages" and are objectionable only if unconscionable or if they constitute a clog on the right to redeem. In *Noakes v. Rice* (1902), a clause that the mortgagor would not sell any beers other than those of the mortgagees in his public house for the 26 years of the mortgagor's lease was held to be oppressive: *cf. Biggs v. Hoddinott* (1898), where on similar facts but for a period of five years, the clause was deemed to be valid.

2. As a general rule any collateral advantage must cease when the mortgage is redeemed: *Bradley v. Carritt* (1903), though in *Kreglinger v. New Patagonia Meat and Cold Storage Co. Ltd* (1914) the court again affirmed their reluctance to interfere with commercial contracts and upheld in its entirety a clause in a mortgage by way of floating charge which provided that the mortgagors could not sell any animal skins to anyone other than the mortgagees, who agreed to pay the full market price, such agreement to last for five years.

Such clause was valid for the full five years even though the mortgage was paid off after two-and-a-half years. The court here felt that the collateral advantage was a separate and independent agreement outside the terms of the mortgage and as such capable of continuing in force after the mortgage had been redeemed.

3. A clause in a mortgage which ties repayments by way of an index-linking arrangement to the value of the Swiss franc is not unconscionable even though it may require a substantial rise in repayments: *Multiservice Bookbinding Ltd v. Marden* (1978). However, where a property company sold a house to a mortgagor of limited means by requiring a premium which amounted to a rate of interest of 57 per cent. per annum the court declared this to be an unreasonable collateral advantage: *Cityland and Property (Holdings) Ltd v. Dabrah* (1968).

Consumer Credit Act 1974

This statute gives the courts a power to reopen any extortionate credit agreement so as to do justice between the parties: sections 137–140. The court will look at interest rates, the debtor's personal attributes, financial pressures and the degree of risk accepted by the creditor together with other various factors likely to be material. The decision in *Ketley v. Scott* (1981) illustrates the application of these provisions. Here the court refused relief where the mortgagor was an experienced businessman, legally advised, who wanted to complete a house purchase the same day and agreed to pay 12 per cent. interest for three months (48 per cent per annum). *Cf. Davies v. Directloans* (1986), were an interest rate of 25.8 per cent. was deemed reasonable because of the degree of risk involved in the venture; in *Woodstead Finance Ltd v. Petrou* (1985), an interest rate of 46 per cent. although held to be "very harsh" was not deemed "extortionate" because of "an appalling record of repayment."

Undue influence

A bargain entered into where a mortgagee has exercised undue influence on the mortgagor may be set aside on equitable grounds: *National Westminster Bank v. Morgan* (1985); *Bank of Baroda v. Shah* (1988). The law in this area has been reviewed recently in *Barclays Bank v. O'Brien* (1994) and *CIBC Mortgages v. Pitt* (1993). The need for the mortgagor to take independent advice has been stressed.

Extinguishment of the right to redeem

1. The right to redeem may be lost:
(a) on sale by the mortgagee;

(b) where a foreclosure decree has been made;

(c) under the Limitation Act 1980, where the mortgagee has been in the possession of the mortgaged land for 12 years;

(d) where the mortgagor has surrendered his equity of redemption to the mortgagee.

2. On redemption a formal reconveyance is no longer necessary and a receipt indorsed on the mortgage deed will discharge the mortgage: L.P.A. 1925, s.115.

Other rights of the mortgagor

1. The right to bring actions against third parties and even against tenants: L.P.A. 1925, s.98.

2. The right to compel transfer of the benefit of the mortgage when the mortgagor is entitled to redeem: L.P.A. 1925, s.95(1).

3. The right to grant leases where the mortgagor is in actual possession of the property: L.P.A. 1925, s.99.

4. The right to accept surrender of leases: L.P.A. 1925, s.100.

5. The mortgagor can apply to the court for the property to be sold even where the mortgagee opposes this. The court in exercising its discretion under section 91(2), L.P.A. 1925 will order a sale where it is just and equitable to do so: *Palk v. Mortgage Services Funding plc* (1993); *Cheltenham and Gloucester B.S. v. Norgan* (1996); *Cheltenham and Gloucester B.S. v. Krausz and another* (1997).

RIGHTS OF THE MORTGAGEE (REMEDIES)

Where a mortgagor defaults under the terms of the mortgage the mortgagee is given various remedies. Sale, foreclosure and suing on the personal covenant are designed to recover capital whilst the appointment of a receiver and taking possession are primarily designed to recover interest.

Sale

1. The power of sale *arises* under L.P.A. 1925, s.101 in a mortgage which shows no contrary intention and:

(a) the mortgage is made by deed (this includes all legal mortgages); and

(b) the legal redemption date has passed, *i.e.* when the mortgage money has become due. If the mortgage is by instalment this arises as soon as any instalment is in arrear.

2. The power of sale becomes *exercisable* under L.P.A. 1925, s.103 in any one of three situations:

(a) where notice requiring payment of the mortgage money has

been served and default for three months (capital payments);
(b) some interest under the mortgage is two months in arrears and unpaid;
(c) on breach of some provisions in the L.P.A. 1925 or in the mortgage (other than for repayment of mortgage money or interest).

Where the power of sale has arisen (section 101) the mortgagee can give title to a purchaser free from the equity of redemption even if the power of sale has not become exercisable (section 103). Consequently, a purchaser need only verify that the power of sale has arisen and this can usually be done by inspection of the mortgage deed: L.P.A. 1925, s.104.

3. The effect of a sale is to vest the whole estate of the mortgagor in the purchaser subject to any prior mortgages but free from the mortgage of the vendor/mortgagee and all subsequent mortgages and free from the equity of redemption. After the sale the money is held on trust to pay in order:
(a) any prior mortgages (if this is agreed);
(b) expenses of the sale;
(c) principal, interest and costs of the vendor's mortgage;
(d) residue to the person entitled to the mortgaged property (including subsequent mortgagees of whom notice has been acquired): *Halifax B.S. v. Thomas* (1995).

4. Duties of the mortgagee on sale: a mortgagee does not usually need a court order to execute sale and with the exception of building societies a mortgagee is not a trustee for the mortgagor. Although he must act in good faith he need not, *e.g.* delay the sale to obtain a better price, nor is a mortgagee negligent if he delays sale provided it is not excessive in the circumstances; *Waltham Forest L.B.C. v. Webb* (1974). The mortgagee need not advertise or attempt to sell by auction. Sale at a low price will not be interfered with in the absence of fraud or bad faith and the mortgagee's motive, *e.g.* spite is immaterial: *Cuckmere Brick Co. Ltd v. Mutual Finance Ltd* (1971)—a mortgagee must obtain a true market value. *Cf. Bank of Cyprus v. Gill* (1980)—a mortgagee must get the best available price. A mortgagee cannot sell to himself: *Tse Kwong Lam v. Wong Chit Sen* (1983). An application of the mortgagee's duties on sale can be seen from *Parker-Tweedale v. Dunbar Bank plc* (1990). However, the Privy Council in *Downsview Nominees Ltd v. First City Corp.* (1992) have recently retreated from a wide formulation of the duty on sale by providing that a mortgagee on sale does not owe a duty of care in negligence to later incumbrancers or the mortgagor himself when exercising the power of sale. The duty owed is founded on equitable

principles, so that the mortgagee must act in good faith to secure
what money is owing but that is so even if this has undesirable
consequences to the mortgagor or later mortgagees.

Foreclosure

Foreclosure is the counterpart of the equitable right to redeem
and amounts to a confiscation of the mortgagor's interest in the
property. In a foreclosure action the court declares that the mortgagor's equitable right to redeem is extinguished and the mortgagee becomes owner at law and in equity.

1. A court order is essential: the mortgagee must initiate proceedings and is granted a foreclosure order *nisi, i.e.* the mortgagor
will lose his property unless he repays what is due on or before a
specified date (generally six months hence). In default the order
is made absolute.

2. In proceedings any "person interested," namely the mortgagor
or subsequent mortgagee, may apply for sale rather than foreclosure: L.P.A. 1925, s.91. In general the court is reluctant to order a
foreclosure: *Palk v. Mortgage Services Funding* (1993).

3. The foreclosure order may be reopened even after it has been
made absolute if, for example, the mortgagor is prevented at the
last moment from obtaining the money, or there is a marked dis-
crepancy between the value of the property and the amount owing.
Note—the court has wide powers to adjourn proceedings in foreclosure actions as well as being able to suspend orders: Administration
of Justice Act 1973, s.8(3).

4. The right to foreclose arises whenever the legal redemption
date has passed or the equitable right to redeem has arisen.

Possession

1. The mortgagee's right to take possession is automatic because
the mortgage gives a legal estate in possession and is exercisable
even if the mortgagor is not in default: L.P.A. 1925, s.95(4); *Four
Maids Ltd v. Dudley Marshall Properties Ltd* (1957), and even if the
mortgagor was not aware of the mortgagee's rights: *Equity & Law
Home Loans v. Prestridge* (1992). However, the court has the power
to restrain any unjust use of the right to possession: *Quennell v.
Maltby* (1979). Possession may of course include receipt of rents
and profits from tenants.

2. Where a mortgagee takes possession equity makes him
account strictly on the footing of wilful default, *i.e.* he must account
not formerly what he did receive, but also for what he ought to
have received if he had managed the property with due diligence.

If the mortgagee takes possession personally he is liable for a fair occupation rent. If he leases the property he must get the best possible rent: *White v. City of London Brewery* (1889).

3. A court order is essential before possession can be obtained and on an application under a mortgage of a dwelling-house the court has a discretionary power to adjourn the proceedings or to grant a stay of execution of any order if it seems likely that within a reasonable time the mortgagor will be able to pay any mortgage instalments due or be able to remedy any other breach of the mortgage: Administration of Justice Act 1970, s.36; A.J.A. 1973, s.8: *First National Bank v. Syed* (1991). These statutory provisions apply whether or not the mortgagor has defaulted on the mortgage: *Western Bank v. Schindler* (1977); the courts interpretation of what is a reasonable time will vary from case to case: *National and Provincial Bank v. Lloyd* (1996); *Cheltenham and Gloucester B.S. v. Norgan* (1996).

4. A mortgagee in possession has the following powers:

(a) to cut and sell timber: L.P.A. 1925, s.101;

(b) the same powers of leasing as a mortgagor in possession: L.P.A. 1925, s.99(2);

(c) the same powers to accept surrenders of leases: L.P.A. 1925, s.100(2).

5. In the context of the matrimonial home a mortgagee may not be entitled to possession in competition with a beneficiary behind a trust: *Williams & Glyn's v. Boland* (1981); *Kingsnorth Finance v. Tizard* (1986).

Appointment of a receiver

1. This is the appointment of a person with management powers who may collect rents and profits and although appointed by the mortgagee he is, in fact, an agent of the mortgagor, which circumvents the "wilful default" problem. Such a remedy is most commonly used where the mortgagor has leased the property and rents and profits can thereby be intercepted.

2. The power to appoint a receiver arises and is exercisable as with a power of sale and a mortgagee already in possession may appoint a receiver. Such appointment must normally be in writing: L.P.A. 1925, s.109.

3. The receiver must apply any money received in the following order:

(a) payment of rent, rates and taxes;

(b) payment of interest on any incumbrances having priority to the mortgage;

(c) the receiver's commission, premiums and cost of repairs;

(d) interest on the mortgage;

(e) if the mortgage so directs in writing, payment towards the discharge of the principal sum otherwise any surplus to the person "best entitled" (*e.g.* the mortgagor).

Right to sue on the personal covenant

1. A mortgage normally contains a specific covenant by the mortgagor to repay the money on a specified date. The mortgagee can sue on this covenant and satisfy judgment out of any of the mortgagor's property. This right is barred after 12 years under the Limitation Act 1980 (six years if not a mortgage by deed). Whenever a payment is made or a written acknowledgment of liability is given by the mortgagor the period begins afresh.

2. The above remedies are in general cumulative; for example, if sale realises less than the mortgage debt then the mortgagee may sue on the personal covenant; or if in possession, a receiver may be appointed. One exception is foreclosure, which puts an end to the other remedies.

The rights of equitable mortgagees

An equitable mortgagee may exercise some of the above remedies.

1. Sale. Only if the mortgage is made by deed, or formerly where a deposit of title deeds was accompanied by a memorandum under seal. The power to sell the legal estate can be acquired by inserting a power of attorney in the deed or by a declaration of trust by the mortgagor empowering the mortgagee to appoint a new trustee of the legal estate. The court may, however, order a sale under an equitable mortgage, even if it is created informally: L.P.A. 1925, ss.90, 91.

2. Foreclosure. This is the primary remedy of an equitable mortgagee. Here the court will order the mortgagor to convey the legal estate.

3. Possession. The mortgagee has no right at law since he possesses no legal estate but it is perhaps possible under the general rule in *Walsh v. Lonsdale* (1882). An equitable mortgagee cannot collect rents without a court order since he does not have the legal reversion.

4. Receiver. A statutory power exists if the mortgage was made by deed although the court can make an appointment where no deed exists.

5. Sue on the personal covenant. The mortgagor can be sued personally for the recovery of the debt.

Other rights possessed by mortgagees

1. The right to lease and accept surrenders: L.P.A. 1925, ss.99, 100.

2. The right to fixtures.

3. The right to possession of the title deeds: L.P.A. 1925, ss.85–86, and an obligation to redeliver on redemption.

4. The right to insure the property: L.P.A. 1925, ss.101, 108.

5. The right to tack further advances: in certain circumstances a mortgagee may demand repayment of several loans in priority to lenders who made loans before the mortgagee's further loans. This is a method of altering the basic rule on priority of mortgages: L.P.A. 1925, s.94.

6. The right of consolidation: this applies where there are mortgages of more than one property. It is the right of a person in whom two or more mortgages are vested to refuse to allow redemption of one without redemption of the others. The right will not exist unless the following conditions can be satisfied: (assume there are two mortgages):

(a) the right to consolidate must expressly be given in one of the mortgage deeds, thereby excluding L.P.A. 1925, s.93(1);

(b) the legal redemption dates on both mortgages must have passed;

(c) both mortgages must have been made by the same mortgagor;

(d) at some stage both mortgages must have been vested in one person and at the same time both equities of redemption must be vested in another's hand. This is termed the simultaneous union of mortgages and equities.

10. LICENCES

Introduction

A licence is a permission to do some act which would otherwise be unlawful in regard to the land of another person. It prevents what otherwise would be a tort, *i.e.* trespass. In general licences lack the qualities of interests in land, namely they are not transferable and will not be enforceable against third parties; however, in the period since the Judicature Act 1875 and particularly in the last two decades the nature and characteristics of certain licences have changed and developed so that they are more akin to interests in land:

> "a new chapter of the law of real property has been opening, in which licences have been held to be protected against revocation not only by the licensor but also by the licensor's successors in title." (Megarry and Wade, *The Law of Real Property*.)

The subject-matter of licences is extensive, though particular areas of interest in recent times have been the overlap with leases, easements and life interests, the decision in *Street v. Mountford* (1985), highlighting the complexity of the use of licences as a method of circumventing the rent legislation regarding security of tenure.

CLASSIFICATION OF LICENCES

An attempt to classify licences according to their enforceability has created a somewhat artificial classification:

(a) bare licences;
(b) a licence coupled with an interest;
(c) contractual licences;
(d) licences protected by estoppel.

Bare licences

Where the licensee provides no consideration, even if made by deed, the licence is a bare licence and is revocable at any time provided reasonable notice is given: *Re Hampstead Garden Suburb Institute* (1995). Damages may be claimed where reasonable notice of revocation is not given. Examples of a bare licence would include the permission to play games in a field, or a permission to camp.

Licences coupled with an interest

This arises where a licence is granted ancillary to the granting of some proprietary right in the land or chattels on the land. The right to hunt animals, fish, or cut timber may all require an attendant permission to enter the land. The right is irrevocable and will bind a purchaser who takes with notice of it. Such interest may be legal as a *profit à prendre* under L.P.A. 1925, s.1(2)(*a*) or enforceable in equity, provided it is registered.

Contractual licences

1 This arises where a licence is granted under the terms of a contract and valuable consideration has been given, *e.g.* admission to a cinema or sportsground in return for payment. Originally, at common law, such licence could be revoked at any time, the licensor's only remedy being a claim in damages if revocation amounted to breach of contract. In recent times the courts have been more willing to grant equitable remedies:

(a) *Winter Garden Theatre (London) Ltd v. Millenium Products Ltd* (1948): *obiter* statement that an injunction may be used to preserve the sanctity of a bargain.

(b) *Hurst v. Picture Theatres Ltd* (1915): specific performance of a contract for wrongful ejection from a cinema after paying for a ticket was the plaintiff's entitlement, as well as having an action for assault; *cf. Wood v. Leadbitter* (1845), where damages only were available.

(c) *Verrall v. Great Yarmouth B.C.* (1980): specific performance of a contract for the hire of a hall was granted, and the purported revocation by the council, in breach of contract, was resisted.

2. Whether a contractual licence binds third parties is unclear on the cases, the initial proposition being that a contractual licence is merely a contract and not an interest in land and cannot bind third parties: *King v. David Allen* (1916). This basic principle has been questioned in recent years and it has been suggested in certain cases that contractual licences are enforceable against third parties unless they are bona fide purchasers for value of a legal estate who have no notice of the interest:

(a) *Errington v. Errington* (1952): a licence to occupy a house in consideration of paying mortgage instalments was binding on the heir of the deceased licensor. The decision has been frequently criticised: see *National Provincial Bank v. Ainsworth* (1965), and a better explanation of the case may be the principle of estoppel.

(b) *Binions v. Evans* (1972): a widow of an ex-employee was permitted to live in a cottage rent free for life on condition she maintained the property. It was held that she had a contractual licence which bound a purchaser who acquired the property with express notice of the interest.

(c) *Tanner v. Tanner* (1975): a mother was held to have a contractual licence to allow her to live in the property until her children were 18, the father having specifically bought the house for the mother and children and the mother having given up possession of a protected tenancy of a flat.

3. In certain cases the courts have provided that a contractual licence gives rise to a constructive trust by virtue of which the licensor cannot turn out the licensee: *Bannister v. Bannister* (1948); *D.H.N. Food Distributors Ltd v. London Borough of Tower Hamlets* (1976), though the extent and usage of this concept is uncertain.

4. The extent and exact nature in terms of enforceability of a contractual licence is a matter of substantial debate. The courts seem to use the concept as a mechanism to achieve a fair and just result and then to try to fit that outcome into accepted legal categories, which it is not always easy to do. In effect, the courts may have produced a new concept known as the "equitable licence," which is akin to an interest in land in that it is irrevocable and enforceable against third parties: *Errington v. Errington*; *Binions v. Evans*; and *Hardwick v. Johnson* (1978) all reinforce this view, though Lord Scarman in *Chandler v. Kerley* (1978) was more sceptical and in *Bristol and West B.S. v. Henning* (1985) the Court of Appeal refused to recognise the existence of any protected equitable interest. A return to the more orthodox view that contractual licences are personal to the parties and not proprietary in nature can be seen from the Court of Appeal decision in *Ashburn Anstalt v. Arnold* (1988), where it was held that a contractual licence was not an interest "subsisting in reference" to land for the purpose of s.70(1) of the Land Registration Act 1925. The Court of Appeal also emphasised that there is no general proposition that when a person sells land and stipulates that the sale should be subject to a contractual licence, a constructive trust will be imposed upon the purchaser. The conscience of the estate owner must be affected. There needs to be very special circumstances showing that the transferee of the property undertakes a new liability to give effect to provisions for the benefit of third parties. The conscience of the transferee has to be affected in a way which gives rise to an obligation to meet the legitimate expectations of the third party: *I.D.C. Group Ltd v. Clark* (1992).

Licences protected by estoppel

1. By extending the principle of estoppel to licences the courts have substantially widened the ambit of licences in recent years. If an owner of land permits, promises or acquiesces to the use of

land by another he may be estopped from denying that person's right to use the land. If the promisor having led the promisee to believe that he will be allowed to stay on the land influences the promisee into spending money, the promise or acquiescence plus the expenditure creates an equity which protects the licence. In *Willmott v. Barber* (1880), Fry J. laid down a set of criteria to be satisfied before a proprietary estoppel arises:

(a) the plaintiff must have made a mistake as to his legal rights;
(b) the plaintiff must have expended some money or done some act on the faith of his mistaken belief;
(c) the defendant must know of the existence of his own right which is inconsistent with the right claimed by the plaintiff;
(d) the defendant must know of the plaintiff's mistaken belief of his right;
(e) the defendant must have encouraged the plaintiff in his expenditure of money or in the other acts which he has done either directly or by abstaining from asserting his legal right.

2. These criteria have by no means been universally applied in the cases and in recent decisions the courts have preferred a wider approach concentrating mainly on the unconscionable behaviour of the promisor: *Crabb v. Arun D.C.* (1976): e.g. *Maltharn v. Maltharn* (1994), where *Willmott v. Barber* was strictly applied.

3. The principle of proprietary estoppel has been applied in many and varied situations in licence cases, and has proved of a particular use because it can be used as a "sword" as well as a "shield," *i.e.* it can found a cause of action as well as a defence:

(a) *Dodsworth v. Dodsworth* (1973): expenditure by a young couple of £700 on improvements to a bungalow, after being encouraged and induced by the promisor that they could live there as their home for as long as they wished, created an estoppel allowing occupation until the expenditure had been reimbursed.
(b) *Pascoe v. Turner* (1979): a widow left in a house she had shared with her lover, who had purchased the property, had been told by him that the house and everything in it was hers. On the strength of this she expended money on repairs and improvements. An estoppel was created and it was ordered that the fee simple be conveyed to her.
(c) *Inwards v. Baker* (1965): a father encouraged his son to build a bungalow on his (father's) land. The court held that the son had a right to occupy the land for as long as he wished. See also *Dillwyn v. Llewellyn* (1862), where, on similar facts, a conveyance of the fee simple to the son was ordered.

(d) *Crabb v. Arun D.C.* (1976): a promisor assured a promisee that he would be allowed a right of access across the promisor's land. In reliance on this statement the promisee sold other land which would have provided an alternative access. The promisor was estopped from denying the right of access.

(e) *Coombes v. Smith* (1986): a young couple who were married to different partners decided they wanted to live together. The man purchased a house. The woman became pregnant and gave up her job. The man did not move into the house, but paid all the bills. The woman decorated the house several times and improved the garden. The man promised that he would always look after the woman, though he refused to put the house in joint names. The relationship ended and the woman claimed an interest in the house. The court held that there was no contractual licence, as no consideration was provided and the woman could not establish an equity as she had not acted to her detriment.

4. Once an equity has been established, the court will satisfy it by using the most appropriate method. Recent cases have utilised the following procedures:

(a) By enforcing the terms of a contract or a lease previously agreed: *J.D. Developments Ltd v. Quinn* (1992).

(b) Perfecting an oral gift, and ordering the transfer of title to the property: *Voyce v. Voyce* (1991).

(c) Declaring one of two joint tenants to be the sole beneficial owner: *Lim Teng Huan v. Ang Swee Chuan* (1992).

(d) Granting a refund of the cost of any expenditure plus interest: *Burrows v. Sharp* (1991).

(e) Estoppel of a claim to occupation by way of adverse possession: *Colchester B.C. v. Smith* (1992).

5. There is no direct authority as to whether the benefit of an estoppel licence can be transferred; it may depend upon the circumstances and construction of the licence itself. It may be personal, as in *Inward v. Baker* (1965)—for life, or be intended to run with the land as in *E. R. Ives v. High* (1967), where a right of way orally given in return for allowing the encroachment of foundations created a right of estoppel, there being no legal interest within L.P.A. 1925, s.1(2)(*a*) which bound any purchasers of the legal estate of the promisor with actual notice. The court here relied on the doctrine in *Halsall v. Brizell* (1957), that he who takes the benefit is subject to the burden. The principle in *E. R. Ives v. High* was approved in *Thatcher v. Douglas* (1995).

6. In the case of registered land, occupation licences may consti-

tute overriding interests under the Land Registration Act 1925, s.70(1). They may also be protected by the entry of a notice or caution on the licensor's registered title.

7. A licence can be determined in accordance with the terms of its grant or by abandonment: *Bone v. Bone* (1992).

11. COVENANTS AFFECTING FREEHOLD LAND

It should at the outset be noted that the rules governing the enforcement of covenants in leases are distinct and separate (see Chap. 5).

If one fee simple owner covenants in favour of another either positively, for example, to construct or maintain a road, or negatively, not to build shops on his land, the question arises as to what extent do these covenants bind the contracting parties and do the benefit and burden of such covenants bind successive owners.

Original parties

As between the original parties to the covenant there is privity of contract and the original covenantee can always enforce the express covenant against the original covenantor, unless the benefit has been expressly assigned to some other person. At Common Law only parties to a deed could sue upon it, but this rule is now qualified by L.P.A. 1925, s.56(1), which provides that "a person may take an immediate or other interest in land ... or the benefit of any ... covenant ... although he may not be named as a party to the conveyance or other instrument". This section seems to allow enforcement by persons other than a party to the deed, provided such persons are identifiable at the time of the deed: *Re Ecclesiastical Commissioners for England's Conveyance* (1936). In order to be within the ambit of section 56 a person must show that the covenant was made *with* him, even though he was not a party to the deed: *Beswick v. Beswick* (1968). Consequently successors in title are outside the ambit of section 56 as they are not ascertainable.

running of covenants

Where a covenant is enforceable by and against successors in title of the original covenantor and covenantee it is said to *run with the land*, *i.e.* the benefit and burden of the covenant is automatically transmitted. In deciding whether a covenant runs with the land there are two sets of principles: the common law rules and the equitable rules, each must be examined separately. The common law rules should be applied first of all, and only if they are inapplicable should the equitable rules be used. The benefit and burden of both positive and negative covenants can pass at common law, but the equitable rules apply only to restrictive covenants.

COMMON LAW RULES—ENFORCEMENT OF COVENANTS BY ASSIGNEE

Benefit of the covenant

For the benefit of the covenant to pass at common law the following conditions must be satisfied:

1. The covenant must *touch and concern the land* of the covenantee, *i.e.* the covenant must not be merely personal in nature (the criteria is similar to that adopted in the cases on landlord and tenant: Chap. 5): see *Smith v. River Douglas Catchment Board* (1949).

2. The covenantee must, at the time of the covenant, have *a legal estate in land* to be benefitted. This is because historically equitable interests in land were not recognised by the common law courts.

3. Up to 1926 the assignee had to have the *same* estate in land as the original covenantee, however this rule has now been modified by L.P.A. 1925, s.78(1), which provides that a covenant is deemed to be made not only with the covenantee but also with his successors in title and persons deriving title under him or them. Consequently persons with a different legal estate, for example, a lease, may now be benefitted as in *Smith v. River Douglas Catchment Board* (1949).

4. The covenant must have been made for the benefit of land owned by the immediate covenantee. No contrary intention should be expressed in the conveyance that the covenant was not intended to run with the land: *Rogers v. Hosegood* (1900).

Burden of the covenant

The basic rule at common law is that the burden of a covenant which affects land does not run with that land; *Austerberry v. Oldham*

Corp. (1885). Consequently enforceability is only possible if the original covenantor retains the land. There is no constructive basis for this rule which has been criticised by the Law Commission in reports in 1965, 1971 and more recently in 1984 in a report on the Transfer of land—the Law of Positive and Restrictive Covenants, which has recommended fundamental changes to this area of law. It suggests the creation of a new species of right known as a land obligation the burden of which could be transmitted with the land. Nevertheless, the principle in *Austerberry v. Oldham Corporation* was re-affirmed recently by the House of Lords in *Rhone v. Stephens* (1994). At present circumvention of the *Austerberry* rule is possible in several ways:

1. Lease the land instead of selling it; enforceability then becomes possible under the privity of estate doctrine.

2. Chain of indemnities: Here the covenantor extracts a covenant of indemnity from his purchaser who in turn will extract the same from any subsequent purchaser until the present occupant is bound. The system may break down on the death or disappearance of the original covenantor, or if there is a break in the chain of indemnities.

3. The doctrine in *Halsall v. Brizell* (1957): If a person wishes to take advantage of a service of facility, for example, to use a road or drains, he must comply with any consequential obligation that goes with it, for example, contributing to the maintenance of the road or drains. The doctrine was applied and reviewed in *Tito v. Waddell (No. 2)* (1977), where the successors in title of a mining company who had acquired rights to remove phosphate from the land had to replant the land with indigenous trees and shrubs.

4. Enlargement of long leases into freeholds: the resulting fee simple being made subject to all the same covenants and obligations as the lease would have been subject to had it not been enlarged: L.P.A. 1925, s.153.

5. Creating an estate rentcharge to secure the payment of money or compel the performance of covenants to repair or build: see Rentcharges Act 1977, s.2.

6. Reserving a right of re-entry on breach of a positive covenant.

EQUITABLE RULES—RESTRICTIVE COVENANTS

The decision in *Tulk v. Moxhay* (1848) created what is known as the modern doctrine of restrictive covenants and enabled the burden of a covenant that was negative in nature to run with the land provided certain criteria had been satisfied. In the case a covenant to maintain the garden on Leicester Square unbuilt upon was enforced by way of injunction against a purchaser of land who was aware of the restriction at the time of the purchase.

Burden of the restrictive covenant

The successors in title of the covenantor will be bound by a restrictive covenant which satisfies the following criteria:

1. The covenant is negative in nature: It is the substance and not the form of the covenant that is crucial. The normal test to be applied is whether or not the covenant is one which involves the expenditure of money for its performance, if it does then the covenant is not negative: *Haywood v. Brunswick Permanent Benefit B.S.* (1881). A covenant which has both positive and negative elements can be severed so that the negative element may be binding on the land: *Shepherd Homes Ltd v. Sandham (No. 2)* (1971).

2. The covenant must be intended by the parties to benefit land retained by the covenantee: Restrictive covenants by analogy with negative easements require in general dominant and servient land. If a covenantee does not own or retain adjacent land capable of benefitting from the restriction the covenant is merely a personal one enforceable between the parties only: *Formby v. Barker* (1903). If the original covenantee parts with his interest, he may only obtain nominal damages against the original covenantor. The sole object of the doctrine of restrictive covenants is to protect enjoyment of the land protected by the covenant: *London C.C. v. Allen* (1914).

3. The covenant must touch and concern the dominant land: This is a question of fact and proximity is essential. In *Kelly v. Barrett* (1924) it was stated that "covenants binding land in Hampstead will be too remote to benefit land in Clapham". The covenant itself must either affect the land as regards mode of occupation, or it must be such as *per se* and not merely from collateral circumstances, affects the value of the land: *Rogers v. Hosegood* (1900). The onus of proof in such cases is on the defendant. In determining what constitutes the dominant tenement, it was held in *Re Ballard's Conveyance* (1937), that the court will not make a severance so as to allow a covenant to be annexed to a part of the land capable of benefitting. In the case, annexation of a covenant to the whole of an estate consisting of 1,700 acres was held to be ineffective since the covenant could not directly benefit the whole of that estate. If a covenant is annexed expressly or impliedly to the "whole and each and every

part" of the dominant land it is enforceable by the successors in title to any part actually benefitting: *Zetland v. Driver* (1939).

4. The burden of the covenant must be intended to run with the land of the covenantor: This may be inferred from the wording of the covenant itself, though in respect of covenants made after L.P.A. 1925, s.79 provides that in the absence of a contrary intention expressed in the conveyance, a covenant is deemed to be made by the covenantor on behalf of himself, his successors in title and the persons deriving title under him or them.

Registration

In terms of enforceability of a restrictive covenant against successors in title to the land a distinction should be made as to whether the covenant was created before or after the coming into effect of the property legislation of 1925.

Covenants made before 1926. These are governed by the doctrine of notice, *i.e.* they bind all persons except a bona fide purchaser for value of the legal estate who has no notice of the covenant. *Note*—the rule in *Wilks v. Spooner* (1911).

Covenants made after 1925. Such covenants are registrable (except those made between landlord and tenant) and are void against a purchaser of the legal estate for money or money's worth unless registered as land charges in the appropriate register: Land Charges Act 1972, s.4(6).

Persons against whom restrictive covenants are enforceable

Where the above rules for enforceability are satisfied, a restrictive covenant becomes an equitable interest, enforceable against all owners or occupiers of the burdened land (except certain purchasers of a legal estate without notice). This applies to any occupier of the burdened land whatever his estate or interest, thus for example, a negative covenant may be enforced by a lessor against an under-lessee. A mere occupier will also be bound; as will a person who obtains title by adverse possession.

Benefit of the restrictive covenant

As between the original parties to the covenants the position is the same as at common law, namely, that privity of contract operates and the covenantee can sue the covenantor. If an assignee of the covenantee wishes to sue he may do so if he can satisfy the common law rules, alternatively he may sue if he can satisfy the special rules devised by equity. Provided a covenant touches and concerns the land of the covenantee, an assignee of the dominant tenement can establish that the benefit of the covenant has passed with land wherever one of the following facts can be established:

(a) That the benefit of the covenant has been effectively annexed to the dominant land.
(b) That the benefit of the covenant has been expressly assigned at the time of the sale.
(c) That both plots of land are subject to a scheme of development.

1. Annexation of the covenant. Here it is necessary to show that the wording of the restrictive covenant made it clear that the benefit was intended to be taken by the original covenantee and by subsequent owners. A classic example of annexation can be seen from *Rogers v. Hosegood* (1900), by the following wording: "with intent that the covenants may enure to the benefit of the vendors . . . their heirs and assigns and others claiming under them to all or any of their lands adjoining . . .". However, to covenant merely with the "vendors, their heirs, executors, administrators and assigns" is insufficient for there is no reference to any land and no particular purpose specified. If the covenant is annexed to the land it runs automatically with that land even if the successor to the land does not know it exists when he takes the conveyance. A successor to a part of land must show that the benefit is annexed to that part: *Formby v. Barker* (1903). In *Re Ballard's Conveyance* (1937), it was provided that there can be no annexation if the area of the dominant tenement is greater than can be reasonably benefitted. To be certain of annexation the covenant should be annexed to the whole, or any part or parts of the dominant tenement: *Zetland v. Driver* (1939).

Statutory annexation. The problems of annexation by express words in the conveyance has now been removed to a great extent by the decision in *Federation Homes Ltd v. Mill Lodge Properties Ltd* (1980) (C.A.), which provided that L.P.A. 1925, s.78 was more than a provision of statutory shorthand for conveyancers and its purpose was to assist annexation. Section 78 enacts that: "a covenant relating to any land of the covenantee shall be deemed to be made with the covenantee, and his successors in title and the persons deriving title under him or them, and shall have effect as if such successors and other persons were expressed". To give substantive effect to this provision simplifies the rules on the passing of the benefit of a restrictive covenant in that it creates a statutory annexation so that express words are no longer necessary provided the covenant touches and concerns the land. The decision has been criticised by many academic writers who prefer a narrower interpretation of the section. In *Roake v. Chadha* (1983) it was provided that although s.78 stated that a covenant is deemed to be made with the covenantee and his successors in title it doesn't follow that the covenant automatically runs with the land. The covenant still had to be construed as a whole to see whether the benefit of it was annexed. Where the covenant was not qualified in any way annexation could readily be inferred, but where the covenant expressly precluded the benefit from passing, unless it was expressly assigned, due weight had to be given to those words. This decision is questionable in that section 78, by contrast with section 79 makes no exception for a contrary intention within its terms, it automatically annexes the benefit regardless of the terms of the covenant.

2. Express assignment of the covenant. The benefit of the covenant will pass if it can be shown that by a separate but contemporaneous document the covenant has been expressly assigned to the assignee.

(a) Transfer by legal assignment as a chose in action is possible under L.P.A. 1925, s.136.

(b) Assignment under the equitable rules as laid down in *Re Union of London and Smith's Bank Ltd's Conveyance, Miles v. Easter* (1933), is also possible. See *Newton Abbot Co-operative Society Ltd v. Williamson and Treadgold Ltd* (1952).

(c) There is conflicting judicial opinion as to whether an express assignment of the benefit of a restrictive covenant annexes it to the dominant tenement so as thereafter to automatically run with the land. Compare *Renals v. Cowlishaw* (1878) which suggests it does, with *Re Pinewood Estate* (1958) which indicates that a chain of assignments is necessary.

As a consequence of the decision in *Federated Homes Ltd v. Mill Lodge Properties Ltd* (1980) the significance of express assignments will diminish in that it will be necessary in fewer instances to establish that the benefit has been expressly transmitted. Compare *J. Sainsbury plc v. Enfield L.B.C.* (1989).

3. Scheme of development. Where an area of land is

developed, for example, for a building scheme, the creator of the scheme may require that the purchasers of each plot shall enter into a number of covenants to maintain the quality of the estate. Where such a scheme exists the purchaser or his assignees can sue and be sued on the mutual obligations. Such a scheme creates a "local law" binding on all owners, irrespective of when the various plots were sold. The following principles for the existence of a scheme were laid down in *Elliston v. Reacher* (1908):

(a) both parties must derive title under a common vendor;

(b) the common vendor, before selling to either party, laid out the estate, or defined parts thereof, for sale in lots subject to restrictions intended to be imposed on all the lots and which, though varying from lot to lot, are consistent only with a general scheme of development;

(c) the restrictions were intended by the common vendor to be and were for the benefit of all the lots intended to be sold; and

(d) the parties to the action, or their predecessors in title purchased their lots from a common vendor on the footing that the restrictions were for the benefit of the other lots in the general scheme: see *Re Wembley Park Estate* (1968).

To an extent these conditions overlap, but the basic requirement is that there is in existence common regulations obviously intended to govern the area of the scheme. In recent times there has been a relaxation of the formal requirements in *Elliston v. Reacher* (1908), so that a scheme was held to exist in *Re Dolphin's Conveyance* (1970) even though there was no common vendor and no lotted estates. Similarly in *Baxter v. Four Oaks Properties Ltd* (1965), a scheme was held to exist even though the common vendor had not laid out the estate in lots prior to the sale. The most important aspect now being to establish an intention to impose a scheme of mutually enforceable obligations in the interests of purchasers and their successors. Community of interest necessarily requires and imports reciprocity of obligations: *Spicer v. Martin* (1888). However, in *Emile Elias & Co. Ltd v. Pine Groves Ltd* (1993) lack of uniformity in the covenants imposed on lots of a similar nature, together with lack of knowledge of all the lots contained within the scheme contributed to the Privy Council holding that no building scheme existed as the necessary intention could not be proved. The general principles governing schemes apply also to sub-schemes, *i.e.* where a lot is subsequently sub-divided. Here the covenants are enforceable, as far as they are applicable, even though none of the purchasers themselves actually covenanted.

Modification and discharge of restrictive covenants

1. It is possible to determine the validity of a restrictive covenant by application to the court for a declaration as to its effect: L.P.A. 1925, s.84(2), as amended by the L.P.A. 1969, s.28(4).

2. A restrictive covenant is permanently discharged where the dominant and servient plots come into common ownership: *Texaco Antilles Ltd v. Kernochan* (1973).

3. A restrictive covenant may be modified or discharged on application to the Lands Tribunal under L.P.A. 1925, s.84(1) who may make a discretionary order wherever:

(a) the restriction is deemed obsolete by virtue of changes in the character of the property or neighbourhood or other material circumstances: *Re Bradley Clare Estates Ltd's Application* (1987); or

(b) that the continued existence of the covenant would impede some reasonable user of the land for public or private purposes, and it confers no practical benefit of substantial value or is contrary to the public interest: *Gilbert v. Spoor* (1983): Compare *Re Edward's Application* (1983);

(c) where the parties entitled to the benefit of the restriction have agreed to its discharge or modification: the parties must be of full age and capacity;

(d) where the proposed discharge or modification will not injure the persons entitled to the benefit of the restriction: *Moody v. Vercan* (1991).

In making any order the Lands Tribunal will take into account any development plan and planning policy for the area.

---

12. PERPETUITIES

CLASSIFICATION OF INTERESTS

In order to understand the perpetuity principle, it is necessary at the outset to understand the distinction between vested and contingent gifts.

Vested in possession. Where a gift gives a present right to present enjoyment (or to rents and profits) this is not a future interest and will not be affected by the perpetuity rule. For example, where Blackacre is conveyed to X for his lifetime.

Vested in interest. Where a gift gives a present right to future enjoyment it is vested for the purposes of perpetuity. The beneficiary is ready to take possession but is merely postponed by the existence of an earlier interest. An interest will be vested for the purposes of the perpetuity rule provided certain criteria has been satisfied:

(a) the person or persons entitled must be ascertained;
(b) the interest must be ready to take effect in possession forthwith, subject only to any prior interests;
(c) the size of the beneficiary's interest must be known (particularly in relation to class gifts). If there is any possibility that a person's share of the property given may vary according to some future event, the whole gift will fail if that event might possibly happen outside the perpetuity period.

Contingent. Such gift gives no right at all unless and until some future event occurs and the conditions above have been satisfied. It is only in relation to contingent interests that the perpetuity rule is invoked.

If Blackacre is given to "X for life; Y for life; remainder to Z in fee simple if he becomes a solicitor," then the nature of the gifts are:

(a) X has an interest vested in possession;
(b) Y has an interest vested in interest;
(c) Z has a contingent interest (if he is not yet a solicitor).

The importance of the difference between vested and contingent gifts is that if it is vested then the gift automatically takes effect, whereas if it is contingent then its operation is uncertain and it may be declared void for perpetuity.

Interests in remainder and in reversion. A reversion is that part of the grantor's interest as is not disposed of by grant, *e.g.* if a grantor creates a life estate "to X for life" the grantor retains the fee simple in reversion, *i.e.* it reverts back at the termination of the life estate. Such reversion operates by law and it is necessarily vested. There can only be one reversion in relation to one estate. A remainder arises where a grantor creates a lessor estate and by the same instrument disposes of some or all of the residue of his estate to one or more persons. If Blackacre is conveyed "to X for life; Y for life; Z in fee simple" then the estates of Y and Z are estates in remainder. Any estate less than a fee simple and upon which a remainder or a reversion (or both) are expectant is known as a "particular estate."

THE PERPETUITY RULE

Introduction 1 The origin of the rule against perpetuities can be traced to the 13th century where the principle was developed that property should not be rendered inalienable. The rule was devised to prevent land being tied up for excessive periods in settlements. The development of the rule was initially common law based culminating in the House of Lords decision in *Cadell v. Palmer* (1833).

2. The rule was amended in minor respects by the L.P.A. 1925 and major changes were introduced by the Perpetuities and Accumulations Act 1964. These statutory reforms were built upon the old law and therefore an understanding of the common law principles is essential, particularly bearing in mind that the 1964 Act is not retrospective and applies only to those limitations coming into effect on or after July 16, 1964.

3. The following steps should be taken in applying the perpetuity rule:
   (a) analyse the nature of the gift into interests in remainder or reversion;
   (b) classify any remainder into vested or contingent (any vested gift is valid);
   (c) apply the common law rule to the contingent interests. If the gift is void at common law;
   (d) apply the provisions of the 1964 Act, provided the limitation took effect on or after July 16, 1964.

The rule at common law

1. Any future interest in any property is void from the outset if it may possibly vest after the perpetuity period has expired. The perpetuity period is 21 years after the death of a life or survivor of a number of lives in being, plus any period of gestation.

2. The term *vest* for the purpose of perpetuity means vested in interest. The question always to be asked is "is it possible that the gift may vest more than 21 years after the death of the last surviving life in being?" There is no wait and see opportunity under the common law rule, the law is concerned with possibilities and not probabilities. If there is the slightest possibility that the period may be exceeded regardless of how unlikely, the gift is void.

3. A gift is tested for perpetuity when the instrument of creation comes into effect:
  (a) Will—date of death of the testator;
  (b) *inter vivos* gift—date of execution of the document.

4. The rule applies to all types of propriatory interests. The grant of an easement in fee simple to use all drains "hereafter to pass" under the grantor's adjacent land is void for perpetuity for it may vest in favour of a successor in title to the grant outside the perpetuity period: *Dunn v. Blackdown Properties Ltd* (1961).

5. It is of no consequence that a gift may never vest at all. The rule of perpetuities is only concerned that if it is going to vest at all, will it vest within the perpetuity period. In a gift to "the first daughter of X to marry", X being a bachelor, the perpetuity problem never arises if X never has a daughter.

6. A gift which would normally be void for perpetuity at common law may be saved by the insertion of an express clause confirming the gift's vesting to a valid period. Such a reference must be explicit to achieve this result. The insertion of the term "within the limitations prescribed by law" may be successful: *Re Vaux* (1939), but not "so far as the rules of law and equity will permit": *Portman v. Viscount Portman* (1922).

7. Where there are no lives in being the perpetuity period is 21 years only.

Lives in being at common law

1. Any living person or persons may be chosen (no animals, trees or corporations) provided they are alive at the date of the gift (or *en ventre sa mère*). They must be:
  (a) expressly or impliedly mentioned in the gift: "to the grandchildren of X who attain 21" would have as implied lives in being the children of X;
  (b) measuring lives: those who in some way or another govern the time when the gift is to take effect, though it is not necessary that the person who is a life in being should receive any benefit from the gift.

2. There is no restriction on the number of lives selected, provided it is reasonably possible to ascertain who they are: *Re Villar* (1928), where a period of restriction "ending at the expiration of 20 years from the day of the death of the last survivor of all the lineal descendants of Queen Victoria who shall be living at the time of my death" was held valid. (Approximately 120 lives in being, who were reasonably easy to trace.) Such provisions are known as "royal lives clauses" and may still be valid provided they are practicable.

In the literal sense anyone alive in the world is a life in being but such a reference would be unworkable and thereby inoperative: *Re Moore* (1901)—a gift calculated by reference to the "last survivor of all persons living at my death" was void: see also *Re Leverhulme* (1943).

Future parenthood at common law

1. The common law rule is concerned only with possibilities, regardless of how remote and even if it can be proved, for example, that the birth of further children is a physical impossibility. The common law rule has a stubborn disregard for the facts of life and will not accept this. Consequently, a gift may be rendered void for perpetuity because a life in being may have another child who might satisfy a contingency outside the perpetuity period; it being irrelevant that that life in being is a woman of 80. The concept of the "fertile octagenarian" is illustrated in *Ward v. Van de Loeff* (1924)—a gift void because a woman of 66 was regarded as still capable of child bearing. Similarly a 70-year-old woman in *Jee v. Audley* (1787).

2. Legal impossibilities are recognised at common law so that the fact that it is legally impossible for a legitimate child to be born to a person under the age of 16 (Marriage Act 1949, s.2) was recognised in *Re Gaites W.T.* (1949).

Class gifts at common law

1. Where a class gift exists the composition of the class and the size of the share that each member of that class is to take must be known. A class gift is a gift of property to persons who come within a certain category or description, and whose share is divisible proportionately to the number of persons in the class, *e.g.* "to all the children of X who attain the age of 25".

2. The rule in *Pearks v. Moseley* (1880) is the test for validity at common law. This provides that if a single member of a class may take an interest outside the perpetuity period the whole gift fails even as regards those who have satisfied the contingency in the gift. A class gift cannot be partially good and partially void, gifts are not severable and any taint of remoteness affects the whole class. See *Re Drummond* (1987); *Re Tom's Settlement* (1986).

3. The class closing rule in *Andrews v. Partington* (1791) can operate to save certain class gifts that otherwise would be void. It is a rule of construction which provides that a class can be closed when the first member becomes entitled to claim his share. The operation of the rule can be excluded by the insertion of a contrary inten-

tion in the gift. The effect of the rule is that no one born after the class has closed can enter the class, but any potential members of it already born are included provided they ultimately satisfy the contingency. In a class gift to "all X's grandchildren that attain 21" the class closes when the first grandchild attains 21. Any other grandchildren already born are potentially within the class, those not yet born are excluded. Where a class gift is preceded by a life interest the class cannot close until the death of the tenant for life at the earliest, since only then will the interest be vested in possession: *Re Bleckly* (1951). Where members of a class are to take an interest at birth and no member exists at the time of distribution the class remains open indefinitely.

Age reduction provisions

1. A remainder is often void under the common law rules because the provisions of the gift stipulate the attaining of an age contingency greater than 21. In a gift "to X for life (a bachelor), remainder to his first son to attain 25", the gift would be void at common law because the first son to attain the contingency, not being a life in being, could only do so outside the perpetuity period.

2. The L.P.A. 1925, s.163(1) allows the substitution of the age of 21 for the offending age if the age contingency is the only reason for rendering the gift void at common law and the limitation takes effect after 1926. Thus, in a gift "to X for life remainder to his first son to attain 30", the age of 21 is substituted for 30 and the gift is valid.

Dependent gifts

A limitation is not void merely because it is followed by a further gift which is void. However, a limitation which is subsequent to and dependent upon a void limitation is itself void even though it must vest if at all within the perpetuity period: *Re Hubbard's W.T.* (1963). A dependent gift is one which is intended to take effect only if the prior gift does, or does not itself take effect. An independent limitation on the other hand has its own date of vesting, and the fate of the prior gift affects only the time when it takes effect in possession. In *Proctor v. Bishop of Bath and Wells* (1794), a gift was made in fee simple "to the first of X's sons to become a clergyman, but if X has no such son then to Y for life." X was still alive at the date of the gift. As the gift over to Y was dependent on the gift to X's sons taking effect it was void.

Unborn spouse limitations

A gift to such children as might be living at the death of their last surviving parent is void at common law if one parent is not a life in being. For example, a limitation to "X (a bachelor) for life; remainder to any wife of X, remainder to such of their children as survive them both" creates the potential problem of the unborn spouse. The gifts to X and any wife he marries are valid, but as X may marry a woman unborn at the date of the gift, she would not be a life in being and as such, if she survives X by more than 21 years, this postpones the gift to the children beyond the perpetuity period.

THE PERPETUITIES AND ACCUMULATIONS ACT 1964

1. The common rule against perpetuities defeated many gifts that would have vested within the perpetuity period by having to test them at the date of inception. In order to prevent this "slaughter of the innocents" the 1964 Act introduced the concept of "wait and see" which provided that a gift is to fail only if and when "it becomes established that the vesting must occur, if at all, outside the perpetuity period" and until that time arrives the Act requires the disposition to be treated as if it were not subject to the rule: section 3(1).

2. The provisions of the Act only apply where the gift is void at common law and the instrument creating the gift takes effect after July 15, 1964.

3. As an alternative to royal lives clauses such as in *Re Villar* (1928), section 1 of the 1964 Act provides that an alternative fixed period of not more than 80 years may be expressly specified in the gift. A gift "to my first descendant to marry within 80 years of my death" may impliedly create the same effect, though an express reference "which I specify as the perpetuity period" is safer.

4. The perpetuity period is unaltered for the purposes of the Act, *i.e.* it remains the relevant lives in being plus 21 years, though the period is now subject to the "wait and see" provisions in section 3 and the method of calculating the lives in being is different.

Future parenthood provisions—section 2

The "fertile octogenarian" problem, which rendered certain gifts void because of the possibility of issue being born when from a physical viewpoint such would have seemed impossible, has now been affected by section 2 of the Act. This lays down certain presumptions in relation to child bearing:

(a) a male cannot father a child until he is 14 years old;
(b) a woman is capable of bearing a child only between the ages of 12 and 55.

These presumptions are rebuttable and evidence may be brought to show that a living person will or will not be able to have a child.

Wait and see rule—section 3

The policy of the Act is to provide that gifts which do in fact vest within the perpetuity period are actually valid. Under section 3 once it is established that a gift is void at common law and no statutory period (maximum 80 years) is provided for, then the "wait and see" rule allows the trustees to wait and see what events actually occur and only if it is clear that the gift must vest outside the period will the gift be void.

Lives in being under the Act

1. For the purposes of the "wait and see" rule a statutory category of lives in being is provided in section 3. As well as falling within this list lives in being must:

(a) be alive and ascertainable at the date of the gift;
(b) if a class or description they must not be so numerous as to render it impracticable to ascertain the death of the survivor; *Re Thomas Meadows* (1971).

2. Where there are no lives in being the perpetuity period is 21 years, the same rule as operates under the common law.

3. The statutory lives under section 3(5) are:

(a) the person who made the disposition (donor);
(b) the person to whom or in whose favour the disposition was made (donee). In the case of a disposition to a class, this includes any member or potential member of the class. Where there is an individual disposition to a person taking only on certain conditions being satisfied, any person as to whom some of the conditions are satisfied and the remainder may in time be satisfied is included;
(c) the parents or grandparents of a donee(s) or potential donee(s);
(d) the owner of a prior life interest.

Class gifts under the Act—section 4(4)

The harshness of the rule in *Pearks v. Moseley* (1880) is mitigated by section 4 of the Act and the principle that a class gift cannot be partly good and partly bad has been eliminated. Once the "wait and see" rule has been applied, only if it becomes apparent that there are potential members of the class whose interests may vest outside the perpetuity period will the gift be void, *i.e.* the gift is valid as regards those who actually fall within the perpetuity period.

Age reduction provisions—section 4(1)

The provision in section 4(1) replaces L.P.A. 1925, s.163 in respect of gifts made after July 15, 1964. If the disposition is not saved by the "wait and see" rule and the disposition is void because of reference to an age contingency greater than 21, then the section operates to replace the offending age with the nearest age which will prevent the disposition being void for perpetuity. Consequently, 21 is not automatically substituted for the offending age. The age will vary according to the respective ages of potential beneficiaries. In a gift to "all the children of X who shall attain the age of 30" and X dies leaving three children aged three, two and one years respectively, it may be necessary to reduce the age contingency to 24, 23 and 22 in respect of the three children, though an alternative view is that the age contingency is reduced to 22 for all of them.

Dependent gifts—section 6

Section 6 of the Act abolishes the common law rule on dependency and a gift will not be void for remoteness by reason only that it is ulterior to and dependent upon an earlier void gift. Each gift is treated as separate and distinct and the perpetuity period applied individually.

The unborn spouse provisions—section 5

In the classic unborn spouse disposition to "A (a bachelor for life); remainder to any wife of A for life; remainder to such of their children as survive them both," such gift to the children would be void at common law, but if the gift is made after the 1964 Act comes into operation it is saved by section 5. This allows the "wait and see" provisions to potentially save the gift, but if the gift does not vest within the period (*i.e.* if A's widow survives him by more than 21 years) then the section operates to convert the gift into a gift to the children then living, even if some of them later predecease the widow.

Exceptions to the perpetuity rule

(a) Interests following an entailed interest in land.

(b) Charities.

(c) Covenants for renewal in a lease.

(d) Mortgages: the rule does not apply to the postponement of a mortgagor's right to redeem.

(e) Restrictive covenants.

(f) Options relating to land: *e.g.* an option to purchase: 1964 Act, s.9.

(g) Rights of entry connected to leases and rentcharges; 1964 Act, s.11.

(h) The right of survivorship under a joint tenancy.

---

13. REGISTRATION OF TITLE

Introduction

The object of registration of title is to make the transfer of land simpler, quicker, cheaper and safer. In unregistered conveyancing on a conveyance of property the vendor's aim is to produce documentary evidence (title deeds) of past transactions over a period of time so as to raise the overwhelming inference that he is the owner of the estate he is purporting to sell. Registered conveyancing aims to do away with the requirement of the repeated examination of the title deeds on successive sales, in its place is a register, a search of which gives to a purchaser a description of the land, the name of the registered proprietor, and any third party registrable rights. The purchaser should then have a complete and up-to-date picture of the state of the title, which, if accompanied by a search in the local land charges register, enquiries of the vendor and a physical inspection of the land, should provide adequate protection. However, the system is not perfect in that certain rights are not registrable and may not be easily identifiable by other checks. The system of registered conveyancing is in the process of being completed throughout the country. Since December 1, 1990, the whole of England and Wales has been an area of compulsory registration, so that whenever and wherever a piece of unregistered land is sold, the details will need to be placed on the register.

Principles of registered conveyancing

1. The "mirror" principle: the register is an accurate reflection of the current title and matters affecting the land.

2. The register and not the title deeds reflect the title; the register is a register of titles and not land, and there are several registers reflecting the various legal estates.

3. The "curtain" principle: any interest arising under a trust is kept off the title and does not affect the purchaser. *Cf.* overreaching provisions relating to unregistered title.

4. The "insurance" principle: the state guarantees the title as portrayed by the register and a registered proprietor is protected. Rectification of any errors on the register is possible and any person who suffers loss as a consequence may be indemnified, *i.e.* compensation paid by the registry.

5. The system of registered title does not in general make any substantive changes to land law, *i.e.* it does not affect the pattern of estates and interests which can exist in land. The principles relating to trusts for sale, strict settlements and co-ownership among others are the same as for unregistered land.

Categories of registration

1. Legal estates. The only estates that may be registered from a title aspect are those that are capable of existing at law under L.P.A. 1925, s.1, namely the fee simple absolute in possession and term of years absolute (though the lease must have more than 21 years to run). Certain legal rentcharges are capable of substantive registration, but under a separate title.

2. Minor interests. Certain third party rights affecting the property may be entered on the register against the legal estate. Examples include life interests under a settlement or trust for sale and restrictive covenants.

3. Overriding interests. Interests which bind a registered proprietor whether or not registered and irrespective of the doctrine of notice. There are 12 groups of overriding interests specified in L.R.A. 1925, s.70(1), the most important of which are:

(a) rights of common, *profits à prendre*, rights of sheepwalk, rights of way and other easements, not being equitable easements required to be protected by notice on the register. As a consequence of *Celsteel Ltd v. Alton House Holdings* (1985) and *Thatcher v. Douglas* (1996) equitable easements openly exercised may be protected as overriding interests. *Note*—section 70(1)(*a*) does not include restrictive covenants;

(b) rights acquired or in the course of being acquired under the Limitation Act 1980 (here the registered proprietor holds in trust for the squatter until registration under L.R.A. 1925, s.75);

(g) the rights of every person in actual occupation of the land or in receipt of the rents and profits thereof save where enquiry is made of such person and the rights are not disclosed;

(i) local land charges;

(k) leases for any term or interest not exceeding 21 years granted at a rent without taking a fine. (Contracts for leases and equitable leases are not protected.)

Contents of L.R.A. 1925, s.70(1)(G)

1. The rights protected under this paragraph are wide and diverse and extend to protect individuals who on equitable grounds deserve protection, but whose interests are inappropriate for registration, or if registrable are often informally created and therefore unlikely to be registered by the layman. It is a controversial category which has been the subject of considerable analysis in the cases.

2. Section 70(1)(G) protects the rights of persons in actual occupation, not the occupation itself. The rights must "subsist in reference to land," thus in *Williams & Glyn's Bank Ltd v. Boland* (1981), the House of Lords held that the beneficial interest of an occupying tenant in common (a wife, the legal estate being held by the husband on trust for sale for both of them as tenants in common to the extent of their contributions) fell within the paragraph.

3. Purely personal interests, such as the spouse's right of occupation under the Matrimonial Houses Act 1983, are not within the protection of the section. The position of the contractual licensee is unclear: *National Provincial Bank v. Ainsworth* (1965).

4. The provision does not apply to rights of persons in occupation of land under a strict settlement because these are exclusively minor interests under the Act; section 86(2).

5. Equitable as well as legal interests are included; *e.g.* a right of occupation under an agreement for a lease or option to purchase: *Webb v. Pollmount Ltd* (1966).

6. "Actual occupation" under the section is a matter of fact and requires physical presence: *Hodgson v. Marks* (1971). A wife living with her husband is in "actual occupation," her interest arising

from contributions to the purchase price: *Williams & Glyn's Bank Ltd v. Boland* (1981). "Actual occupation" means some form of established or settled occupation and not a mere fleeting presence: *Abbey National B.S. v. Cann* (1991). Preparatory steps before completion such as carrying out building work may not be sufficient: *Lloyds Bank plc v. Rosset* (1991). Completion is the relevant time for determining whether someone is in "actual occupation" for the purposes of s.70(1)(g).

7. A purchaser can only take free of an otherwise overriding interest if he makes enquiry of the person who holds the interest and the interest is not disclosed. The principal problem for a purchaser is to discover the existence of such person in order to make the relevant inquiries. As to the nature of inquiries to be made: see *City of London B.S. v. Flegg* (1988).

8. The owner of an overriding interest may expressly consent to a sale or mortgage of the land and in so doing lose priority against a purchaser: *Equity and Law Home Loans v. Prestidge* (1992). However, in *Woolwich B.S. v. Dickman* (1996) it was suggested that any waiver by the owner of the overriding interest would need to be entered on the register.

The Register

1. On registration, the registered proprietor is given a "land certificate" which is a representation of title and provides a copy of those parts of the register relating to his land. It is the register which the land certificate represents that is the proof of title, not the certificate itself.

2. The register is divided into three sections:

(a) *the property register*: this describes the land and estate for which it is held, by reference to a plan. It also contains general notes of easements and restrictive covenants which exist for the benefit of the land;

(b) *the proprietorship register*: this specifies the nature of the registered interest, the name and address of the proprietor and any limitations on the registered proprietor's dealing with the land, *e.g.* cautions, inhibitions or restrictions;

(c) *the charges register*: this contains entries of incumbrances adverse to the land, *e.g.* mortgages and restrictive covenants.

Classes of registered title

When land is first registered the nature of the title described in the proprietorship register will depend upon the proof of the title which the estate owner can demonstrate.

1. Absolute title. (Can be acquired by both freehold and leasehold estate owners.) This title is granted where the registrar can verify that the title cannot be successfully challenged. In the case of freehold land it vests in the first registered proprietor, the fee simple in possession, subject to incumbrances and other entries on the register, overriding interests (unless the contrary is stated on the register) and minor interests of which the registered proprietor has notice. An absolute title to leasehold property guarantees that the lease was validly granted, *i.e.* that the superior titles have been investigated.

2. Good leasehold title. Applies only to leases and is granted where the landlord's title has not been investigated. Otherwise it is the same as absolute title.

3. Qualified title. This is the same as absolute title save that it is subject to any defect in the register and registration does not therefore affect the enforcement of the estate or right constituting the defect.

4. Possessory title. Where a possessor of land claims title by adverse possession under the Limitation Act 1980, he may register a possessory title. It is the same as an absolute title but does not affect or prejudice the enforcement of any estate or rights which existed at the time of first registration.

5. Titles can be upgraded. *i.e.* converted from inferior ones into superior or absolute titles, on application to the registrar. For example, freehold possessory title registered for 15 years will be converted to absolute title; leasehold possessory title registered for 10 years will be converted to good leasehold title: L.R.A. 1925, s.77, as amended by Land Registration Act 1986, s.1.

Protection of minor interests

1. All interests that are not registered titles or overriding interests are minor interests which should be protected by registration. Failure to register renders the minor interest void against a purchaser. Protection of a minor interest is effected by one of four methods.

2. Notice in the charges register: this is available if the land certificate is produced at the Registry, *i.e.* it usually requires the agreement of the proprietor. Interests such as estate contracts, options and legal rentcharges will be protected in this way.

3. Caution in the proprietorship register: this entitles the cautioner to be informed of a proposed dealing and gives time to object. It is an "unfriendly" act and is often used if the land certificate cannot be obtained: *Clark v. Chief Land Registrar* (1994).

4. Inhibition. An order of the court or registrar forbidding dealings either indefinitely or until a certain event. It is used mainly in bankruptcy matters or in cases of emergency.

5. Restrictions. This is the most common entry: normally made on the application of the registered proprietor, which prevents dealings unless certain conditions are complied with. It is usually used to protect equitable interests arising under a settlement or a trust of sale.

Registration of title and the doctrine of notice

The object of the land registration system was to free a purchaser from the hazards of the doctrine of notice. Registration was to take the place of the doctrine of notice. The effect of failure to register any registrable interest which is not an overriding interest is that the purchaser takes free of it. (*Note*—the parallel with unregistered land): L.R.A. 1925, s.20. Despite this general principle attempts have been made to reintroduce the doctrine of notice into the sphere of registered land and some doubts have been cast upon the absolute nature of section 20: *Peffer v. Rigg* (1978); *Lyus v. Prowsa* (1982).

The guarantee of title

1. Registered title is often said to be a state guaranteed title, but even if a proprietor has absolute title, there may be situations where, due to error or fraud, a person other than the true owner has been registered and it would be unjust not to alter the register. The L.R.A. 1925 provides a mechanism for rectification where this occurs, and will provide a right of indemnity in favour of a registered proprietor who suffers a loss because of the rectification.

2. *Rectification*: can be ordered under L.R.A. 1925, s.82, as amended by A.J.A. 1977, s.24:

(a) where an entry has been obtained by fraud: *Argyl B.S. v. Hammond* (1984);

(b) to give effect to an overriding interest: *Chowood v. Lyall (No. 2)* (1930);

(c) where by reason of any error or omission on the register or any entry made under a mistake it may be deemed just to rectify the register.

The court has no general discretion to grant rectification merely because it might be thought just to do so. The courts' power is limited to the grounds specified in section 82 of the L.R.A. 1925: *Norwich and Peterborough Building Society v. Steed (No. 2)* (1993).

3. Rectification is not available (except for the purpose of giving effect to an overriding interest or an order of the court) so as to affect the title of a registered proprietor in possession unless:

(a) the proprietor caused or substantially contributed to the error or omissions by fraud or lack of proper care: *Re 139 Deptford High Street* (1951); or

(b) if for any other reason it would be unjust not to rectify against him: *Epps v. Esso Petroleum Ltd* (1923); *Noble v. Ferdinand* (1992)—common mistake of the parties.

4. *Indemnity* can be claimed under L.R.A. 1925, s.83, where there has been:

(a) loss suffered by rectification;

(b) loss suffered by an error in the register which is not rectified;

(c) loss suffered by reason of the loss or destruction of documents lodged at the Registry or by reason of an error in an official search.

No indemnity is payable:

(a) where no loss is suffered by reason of the rectification: *Re Chowood's Registered Land* (1933);

(b) where a claimant obtains rectification (he cannot be awarded an indemnity in addition);

(c) where the applicant or a person through whom he claims other than for value has caused or substantially contributed to the loss by fraud or lack of proper care;

(d) where the claim is statute barred.

5. The amount of compensation is not to exceed:

(a) where the register is rectified, the value of the interest immediately before rectification; or

(b) where no rectification, the value of the interest at the time when the error or omission was made.

14. SAMPLE QUESTIONS AND MODEL ANSWERS

Question 1 (Co-ownership)

G, H, J, K and L, who are all of full age, bought a vacant plot of unregistered land known as "Parker's Piece" from N in 1994 hoping its value would increase. The conveyance, which the parties prepared without professional advice, was sealed by all the parties and purported to convey the land "to G, H, J, K and L as joint tenants in law and equity." The purchasers provided the purchase money equally.

In 1995 K died. In 1996 H purchased J's interest. In 1997 H died, appointing J as his executor. Recently L orally agreed to purchase G's interest in the property for £5,000.

Explain the devolution of the legal estate and of the equitable interests in "Parker's Piece," and advise L how he should protect his interest in the property.

Answer

The conveyance of the property to G, H, J, K and L creates a form of co-ownership, which is where land is conveyed to two or more persons simultaneously.

Such co-ownership creates a trust of land under the provisions of the L.P.A. 1925 and Trusts of Land and Appointment of Trustees Act 1996. The trustees of the co-owned property will hold the legal estate on a joint tenancy for the benefit of the equitable owners.

The 1996 Act converts all existing trust for sale mechanisms into new trusts of land. Consequently when the conveyance was executed in 1994 a trust for sale was created the trustees being under an imperative obligation to sell the land, though they had a power to postpone sale. On January 1, 1997 when the 1996 Act became operative, the trust for sale was replaced with a trust of land under which the trustees have the powers of an absolute owner, subject to any express terms of the trust and exercisable consistent with the provisions of the Law of Property Act 1925 and 1996 Act.

The legal estate is held as an unseverable joint tenancy under the trust of land created by ss.34 and 36 L.P.A. as amended by Part I of the 1996 Act.

In that no trustees are specifically appointed the first four individuals' named in the conveyance who are of full age and capacity will hold the legal estate as trustees. There can be no more than four trustees in this situation—L.P.A. 1925, s.36(1), and Trustee Act 1925, s.34, as amended. Consequently, G, H, J and K will hold the legal estate for the benefit of G, H, J, K and L in equity. In that the conveyance was prepared without professional advice and was sealed, this may operate as a valid deed provided it is also signed and witnessed.

This simplifies conveyancing in that it enables a purchaser to deal only with the trustees and to effectively take free of the interests of the beneficiaries. The nature of a joint tenancy is that none of the parties are deemed to have separate rights as against the outside world. All they have is the potential right to the whole if they are the survivor. The *jus accrescendi* (right of survivorship) operates. It is no longer possible for the legal estate to be held on a tenancy in common.

In terms of the beneficial entitlement to the property it is necessary to decide whether the parties are joint tenants or tenants in common. Traditionally for a joint tenancy to exist the four unities must exist, *i.e.* unity of possession, title, time and interest. In that G, H, J, K and L acquire their rights by way of the 1994 conveyance this implies unity of title and time. They appear to have interests which are the same in extent, nature and duration, and the need for unity of possession has been modified by ss.12 and 13 of the 1996 Act. Consequently the unities appear to be present, which is consistent with both a joint tenancy and a tenancy in common. It is only if one of the unities is missing that it can be concluded that a tenancy in common has been created. In that the conveyance provided that the parties were "joint tenants in law and equity" this will be conclusive as to the status of the parties. The fact that the parties have provided the purchase money in equal shares is consistent with this (presumption). The fact that the parties bought the property hoping its value would increase would indicate a partnership venture, *i.e.* a common venture with a view to profit, and as the *jus accrescendi* has no place in business: *Lake v. Craddock* (1732) this would be consistent with a tenancy in common. However, this is only a presumption and will bow to the evidence to the contrary in the conveyance with the conclusion that the parties are joint tenants in equity.

The effect of K's death in 1995 is that the legal estate will now be held by G, H and J as trustees. Because the legal estate is held on a joint tenancy the survivorship principle operates. As far as the beneficial interests are concerned again survivorship operates as the parties are joint tenants. The remaining parties G, H, J and L now have potential one-quarter shares instead of potential one-fifth shares.

When H purchases J's share this has no effect on the legal estate and J remains a trustee. The effect on the joint-tenancy in equity is that severance takes place by way of the alienation of J's share to H. The unities of title and time are destroyed and consequently H holds one-quarter share on a tenancy in common and the remaining three-quarters is still held on a joint-tenancy for G, H and L.

When H dies in 1997 the survivorship principle operates in respect of the legal estate and G and J hold the legal estate as trustees for the benefit of G and L as to three-quarters on a joint-tenancy (H having lost his potential share by way of survivorship). The other one-quarter share on a tenancy in common which was held by H will now pass by virtue of his will to be held by his executor(s) for the benefit of his estate, the survivorship principle not operating in respect of a tenancy in common.

Recently L orally agreed to purchase G's interest in the property for £5,000. This has no effect on the legal estate but raises the issues as to whether this can amount to a severance of the joint tenancy in equity. In that the agreement is oral it would not appear that there is an enforceable agreement to transfer the share in equity and therefore it cannot be treated as an equitable alienation. Similarly the oral agreement does not comply with L.P.A. section 36(2) which provides that:

> ". . . where a legal estate (not being settled land) is vested in joint tenants beneficially and any tenant desires to sever the joint tenancy in equity, he shall give to the other joint tenants a notice in writing of such desire or do such other acts or things as would in the case of personal estate, have been effectual to sever the joint tenancy in equity."

Whilst the actions of L and G do not expressly come within section 36(2) it is in the nature of the "other acts and things" which incidentally are capable of effecting a severance as evidenced in *Re Drapers Conveyance* (1969) and more recently in *Burgess v. Rawnsley* (1975), where it was held that an oral agreement, in circumstances which clearly indicated that the parties treated themselves as having a share, amounted to a severance. Consequently the joint tenancy as to the three-quarters between G and L would appear to be severed and each party would be entitled to three-eighths of the purchase money.

The final position would appear to be that the legal estate is held by G and J for the benefit of the estate of H as to one-quarter, and three-eighths for G and three-eighths for L (unless the agreement actually takes effect).

L not being a trustee should attempt to have himself appointed such that he may be able to take part in any management decision

relating to the property. If L has the backing of the other beneficiaries an application for appointment can be made under s.36
Trustee Act 1925 and ss.19 and 20 1996 Act. Further, he should
ensure that any severance of the joint tenancy is evidenced on the
face of the conveyance so that in the event of a single trustee
dealing with the legal estate, a purchaser would have to insist on
the appointment of a second trustee in accordance with the terms
of the Law of Property (Joint Tenants) Act 1964 as amended by
the Law of Property (Miscellaneous Provisions) Act 1994.

Question 2 (Leases)

In 1990 K, the fee simple owner of a large agricultural estate,
leased "The Briars," one of several houses on the estate, by deed
to L for 21 years at a rent of £5000 per annum. The lease contained
(*inter alia*) covenants by L to keep "The Briars" in good tenantable
repair and to pay £25 per annum towards the upkeep of the private
roads on K's estate. "The Briars" adjoins a public highway. L
assigned the lease to M in 1992 and M assigned the lease to N in
1993. M has since been adjudicated bankrupt. Explain to K how
he can obtain damages from L or N, and who will be ultimately
liable:

(a) if N allows "The Briars" to fall into disrepair; and
(b) if N refuses to contribute to the upkeep of the roads.

Answer

This question relates to the rules governing the enforceability of
covenants between parties to a lease and their assignees. Significant changes to this area of law have been made by the Landlord
and Tenant (Covenants) Act 1995 which became operative on January
ary 1, 1996. The bulk of the provisions of the Act are not retroactive
and apply only to leases created after the coming into force of the
Act.

Given that the lease in the problem was granted in 1990 the old
rules will govern enforceability.

The relationship between K and L is one of privity of contract
in that they are the original landlord and tenant. The effect of this
is not only that K may enforce all the covenants in the lease against
L, whilst L retains the lease, but also that L remains liable on the
covenants for the whole term, notwithstanding any assignment of
the lease: *Warnford Investments Ltd v. Duckworth* (1979). It would of
course have been open for K and L to restrict their contractual
obligations for the periods when they were respectively to retain
the lease or the reversion.

On the assignment of the lease to M, this creates a relationship of privity of estate between K and M for the duration of the period that M holds the lease. The consequence of privity of estate is that the benefit and burden of all covenants that "touch and concern" the land (*Spencers case* (1583)) or in the phraseology of the L.P.A. 1925, ss.141 and 142, "have reference to the subject matter of the lease" will pass with the land. Any covenant which "affects the landlord in his capacity as landlord or the tenant in his capacity as tenant" (Cheshire) may be said to touch and concern the land. Any covenant which by its nature and not merely through extraneous circumstances affect the nature, quality or value of the land, or the mode of enjoying it, may fall within the definition. Based on the decision in *Williams v. Earle* (1868), a covenant to repair property clearly touches and concerns the land and by analogy the burden of the covenant to keep "The Briars" in good tenantable repair will pass with the land. The covenant to contribute towards the upkeep of the roads on the estate is less easy to classify in that we are told that "The Briars" adjoins a public highway and as a consequence any tenant may not use or have need of the private roads. Covenants to pay rates in respect of other land: *Gower v. Postmaster-General* (1887) and to pay an annual sum to a third person: *Mayho v. Buckhurst* (1617) have been held not to touch and concern the land on the ground that they did not affect the land as such. An analogy may be drawn but no definite conclusion is possible. It must also be noted that for the rule in *Spencers case* to operate the lease must be in due form, which this one is, *i.e.* created by deed and there has to be a legal assignment of the whole term. The nature of the assignments in the question are not specified.

As between K and N there is privity of estate, N being the current tenant. This gives K a dual possibility in terms of his ability to sue. He can attempt to recover from L in privity of contract or sue N directly under privity of estate in respect of those covenants which have passed with the assignment, if any. L and N may both therefore be responsible for breach of the covenants but K can only obtain satisfaction from one, liability is alternative not cumulative: *City of London Corporation v. Fell* (1994).

Since the lease is within the terms of the Leasehold Properties Repair Act 1938 K has a choice of remedy and in serving a section 146 notice may require forfeiture, though the question indicates that only damages are claimed.

In respect of the liability of L and N the primary liability is on the person causing the breach, namely N, though as has been observed K has the choice of suing either L or N. The liability of

M would be restricted to any breaches caused by M during the period in which he held the lease, provided the burden of such covenants had passed.

If K chooses to sue L in privity of contract, a factor which may be motivated by the respective financial status of L and N, the issue of whether L can recover any damages he has to pay is raised. It is usual for an assignor to take a covenant of indemnity from the assignee, thereby guarding against future breaches of covenant. L may have taken such an indemnity from M, but we are specifically informed that M is bankrupt, in which case it may be difficult for M to satisfy any debt. In the absence of any express indemnity the L.P.A. 1925, s.77(1)(c), implies an indemnity in any assignment for value, which may be the case here. This will not solve the problem of M's bankruptcy and an alternative method enabling L to sue N direct needs to be found. The solution would appear to arise under the rule in *Moule v. Garrett* (1872), which on quasi-contractual principles enables a joint debtor, who has paid money to a common creditor for the exclusive benefit of the other co-debtor, to recover direct from that person. Consequently if L pays damages to K in respect of any breach for which N is responsible then by application of this principle L can recover direct from N and need not sue through the chain involving M: *Wolveridge v. Steward* (1833). Where the burden of any covenant has not passed with the assignment then L will be liable for damages and will have no method of recovery.

Note—Had the lease in the problem been created after 1995 then the terms of the new Act would have applied in full. The major change affecting the problem being that the original covenantor would be liable in respect of leasehold covenants (not personal ones) only when the lease was vested in him. This effectively releases any tenant from liability after assignment (Chap. 5 deals with the new changes in full).

Question 3 (Estates and Leases)

Consider the effect of the following limitations in a deed taking effect today:

    (a) to A for one year with an option to renew on the same terms;
    (b) to B for 21 years or until his death, whichever is the earlier;
    (c) to C for 21 years, to commence when C marries.

Answer

    (a) The grant of the property for one year by deed would create a legal term of years absolute within L.P.A. 1925, s.1(1), by virtue of the provisions in L.P.A. 1925, s.52, *i.e.* it is a legal lease for one year initially. The reference to the option to renew on the same term raises the question as to whether this creates a perpetually renewable lease. In order for such a lease to exist there has to be a reference to the renewal clause itself, though this has not always been the case as is highlighted by decisions such as *Parkus v. Greenwood* (1950) and *Northchurch Estates Ltd v. Daniels* (1947). In the latter of these cases an option to renew "on identical terms and conditions" was held to create a perpetually renewable lease. The current view is that the courts lean against the interpretation of a perpetually renewable lease unless there is a specific reference to the renewal clause itself. This is illustrated by the decision in *Burnett v. Barclay* (1980). Consequently, as there is no specific reference here to the existence of the renewal clause, the better view is that this is a single renewal only. Had it been a perpetually renewable lease it would have converted to a term of 2,000 years under the L.P.A. 1922, s.145, and Schedule 15.

A single option to renew is an estate contract and as such is registrable under the Land Charges Act 1972, and must be registered in order to be enforceable against any subsequent purchaser for money or monies worth of the legal estate. The effect of the limitation is, therefore, that A can occupy the property for one year initially with a renewal for a single year.

(b) For a lease to create a legal term of years absolute within L.P.A. 1925, s.1(1), it must be created in the correct manner (*i.e.* by deed, unless it falls within the three-year oral exception created by L.P.A. ss.52 and 54). For any lease to exist, exclusive possession must be given together with the fact that there is certainty of duration. Here a lease is granted for 21 years but is determinable on the dropping of a life. If the lease is at a rent or fine it may fall within L.P.A. 1925, s.149(6), as ". . . a term of years determinable with life or lives . . ." and as such would be converted into a 90-year term: *Skipton B.S. v. Clayton* (1993). If no rent or fine is paid and the lease is gratuitous the section will not apply and the lease will operate as a term for 21 years determinable on B's death. Such a lease cannot be legal as it contravenes the meaning of "absolute" in section 205(1) of the L.P.A. 1925 in that it is determinable on the dropping of a life. Consequently it would be an equitable lease only.

(c) As a pre-requisite of any valid lease there has to be certainty of duration, *i.e.* the maximum duration of the term must be calculable. The problem here is that the lease is to commence on an uncertain event though once it commences there is certainty of duration. An analogy can be drawn with *Askew v. Tarmac Roadstone Holdings* (1991), where a lease containing a commencement date by reference to the date of a planning permission at some future date was held to be too uncertain. It should also be noted that a lease must not contravene L.P.A. 1925, s.149(3), which provides that a lease at a rent limited to take effect more than 21 years from the date of the instrument creating it is void. The question creates the basic problem of uncertainty as to when C marries. If a term of years is fixed by reference to some collateral matter, such matter must either be itself certain or capable of becoming certain before the lease takes effect: *Lace v. Chantler* (1944). Consequently, it may be argued that as it is uncertain when the marriage will take place the lease is void.

Question 4 (Mortgages—Power of Sale of the Mortgage)

In 1990 Hugh borrowed £5,000 from Jack secured by a first legal mortgage of Hugh's unregistered freehold house, Whiteacre. In October 1991 Hugh borrowed a further £3,000 with interest at 12 per cent. from Pam secured by a second legal mortgage on Whiteacre. Hugh has now fallen into arrears with his payments of interest due under the second mortgage. Jack holds the title deeds of Whiteacre.

(a) Explain in what circumstances Pam could sell Whiteacre to secure repayment of her loan and how any such sale would affect Jack's position.

(b) If in the exercise of any power of sale she may have Pam sells Whiteacre at less than its open market value, would Hugh have any remedy against:
   (i) Pam, or
   (ii) the purchaser from Pam?

(c) How must Pam apply the proceeds of any such sale of Whiteacre and what special precautions must she take in doing so?

Answer

(a) A power of sale arises in accordance with L.P.A. 1925, s.101, if the mortgage has been made by deed and the mortgage money is due (provided no contrary intention is shown in the deed). If the mortgage is to be paid by instalment this arises as soon as any instalment is in arrears. The power of sale is exercisable under the terms of L.P.A. s.103, when one of three conditions is satisfied, namely that some interest under the mortgage is at least two months in arrears; that there has been three months' default in repayment of the loan after notice requiring it has been served on the mortgagor or that there has been a breach of some provision in the L.P.A. 1925 or some covenant in the mortgage deed (other than for repayment of mortgage money or interest). It should however be noted that these statutory powers may be varied or extended by the mortgage deed. The question does not indicate the extent of the arrears in the payment of interest under Pam's mortgage, but if that interest is at least two months in arrears, the power of sale has become exercisable. The mortgage is legal and section 101 consequently appears to have been complied with (the legal redemption date often being six months after the creation of the mortgage).

As to Jack's position being a prior mortgagee any sale by Pam is subject to his mortgage: L.P.A. s.104(1), and on a sale he can elect to have his mortgage paid from the proceeds of sale, or alternatively the sale of the property will remain incumbranced by his mortgage.

(b)(i) Pam is not a trustee for the mortgagor, but must act in good faith, however there is no obligation on her to sell by auction or to advertise the property. As a general rule sale at a low price will not be interfered with in the absence of fraud or negligence. If a sale takes place at less than the open market value this raises an inference of lack of good faith and damages may be awarded. In *Cuckmere Brick Co. Ltd v. Mutual Finance Ltd* (1971) where damages were awarded to compensate for a sale of a plot of land where full particulars had not been given, it was stated by Salmon L.J. that ". . . a mortgagee in exercising his power of sale owes a duty to take reasonable precautions to obtain the true market value of the mortgaged property on the date on which he decides to sell."

In *Bank of Cyprus v. Gill* (1979), it was suggested that the mortgagee must get the best available price but this may be overstating the case and in fact in *Downsview Nominees Ltd v. First City Corp.* (1992) the court doubted whether a mortgagee on sale had any duty of care in negligence to later incumbrancers or the mortgagor himself when exercising the power.

If Pam fails to observe any required duty in exercising the sale and sells at an artificially low price, then damages may be payable to Hugh. In *Tomlin v. Lace* (1889), where a mortgagee had misdescribed the property he had to make an allowance to the purchaser from the price and was held liable to the mortgagor for the difference.

Pam could not sell the property to herself either directly or through an agent as this would not be a bona fide sale: *Tse Kwong Lam v. Wong Chit Sen* (1983).

(ii) Once the power of sale has arisen (s.101) the mortgagee can give a good title to the purchaser free from the equity of redemption, even if the power of sale has not become exercisable: L.P.A. 1925, s.104. If the purchaser is aware of any facts showing that the power of sale has not become exercisable or that there is any impropriety in the sale, he will not get a good title.

Consequently, any purchaser from Pam would obtain a good title provided he was not aware that the sale was abnormally low or that there was any fraud, bad faith or impropriety involved.

(c) Pam must pay off the prior mortgage of Jack (if this is agreed) and apply the remainder of the proceeds of sale in accordance with L.P.A. 1925, s.105 which makes Pam a trustee of those proceeds to be applied in the following order:

(a) to pay the expenses of the sale;
(b) to pay the principal sum, interest and costs of the vendor/mortgagee's mortgage;
(c) residue to the next incumbrancer, but if none then to the mortgagor.

Pam must make sure that in paying over the residue it is to the person best entitled. She should check in the relevant register to determine whether any later mortgages have been registered, and if so this amounts to notice to her. If she pays the residue to Hugh without making this inquiry and it transpires that subsequent mortgagees exist there will be liability.

INDEX